Name ______________________

1.

	ASSETS				=	LIABILITIES	+	OWNER'S EQUITY	
	Cash	+	Accounts Receivable	+	Supplies	=	Accounts Payable	+	______, Capital
a.									
b.									
c.									
d.									
e.									
f.									
g.									
h.									
i.									
j.									

2.

T5-BAO-025

Page not used.

Name ______________________

PROBLEM 1 - 2 ___

1. *Omit "00" in the cents columns.*

2. *Omit "00" in the cents columns.*

PROBLEM 1 - 2 ___ , Concluded

3. *Omit "00" in the cents columns.*

Name ______________________________

PROBLEM 1 - 3 ___

1. *Omit "00" in the cents columns.*

2. *Omit "00" in the cents columns.*

PROBLEM 1 - 3 ___ , Concluded

3. *Omit "00" in the cents columns.*

Name ______________________________

PROBLEM 1 - 4 ___

1.

	ASSETS			=	LIABILITIES	+	OWNER'S EQUITY	
	Cash	+	Supplies	=	Accounts Payable	+	________, Capital	
a.								
b.								
c.								
d.								
e.								
f.								
g.								
h.								
i.								

PROBLEM 1 - 4 ___ , Continued

2. *Omit "00" in the cents columns.*

Name ______________________________

PROBLEM 1 - 4 ___ , Concluded

Page not used.

1.

ASSETS							=	LIABILITIES	+	OWNER'S EQUITY
Cash	+	Accounts Receivable	+	Supplies	+	Land	=	Accounts Payable	+	________, Capital
________	+	________	+	________	+	________	=	________	+	________, Capital
		________					=	________	+	________, Capital
		________					=			________, Capital

2.

	ASSETS							=	LIABILITIES	+	OWNER'S EQUITY	
	Cash	+	Accounts Receivable	+	Supplies	+	Land	=	Accounts Payable	+	________, Capital	
a.												
b.												
c.												
d.												
e.												
f.												
g.												
h.												
i.												

3a. *Omit "00" in the cents columns.*

3b. *Omit "00" in the cents columns.*

Name ____________________

3c. *Omit "00" in the cents columns.*

Page not used.

Name ______________________________

PROBLEM 1 - 6 ___

1. *Omit "00" in the cents columns.*

2. *Omit "00" in the cents columns.*

3. *Omit "00" in the cents columns.*

Name ______________________

CONTINUING PROBLEM

1.

	ASSETS					=	LIABILITIES	+	OWNER'S EQUITY	
	Cash	+	Accounts Receivable	+	Supplies	=	Accounts Payable	+	____________, Capital	
a.										
b.										
c.										
d.										
e.										
f.										
g.										
h.										
i.										
j.										
k.										
l.										
m.										
n.										
o.										
p.										
q.										
r.										

CONTINUING PROBLEM, Continued

2. *Omit "00" in the cents columns.*

3. *Omit "00" in the cents columns.*

Name ______________________________

CONTINUING PROBLEM, Concluded

4. *Omit "00" in the cents columns.*

Page not used.

Name ______________________

PROBLEM 2 - 1 ___

1. and 2.

Cash

Accounts Receivable

Supplies

Prepaid Insurance

Automobiles

PROBLEM 2 - 1 ___ , Continued

Equipment

Notes Payable

Accounts Payable

___________________ , *Capital*

Professional Fees

Rent Expense

Salary Expense

Automobile Expense

Blueprint Expense

Miscellaneous Expense

PROBLEM 2 - 1 ___ , Concluded

3.

Trial Balance

Name ______________________________

PROBLEM 2-2 ___

1.

JOURNAL

	DATE	DESCRIPTION	POST. REF.	DEBIT	CREDIT	
1						1
2						2
3						3
4						4
5						5
6						6
7						7
8						8
9						9
10						10
11						11
12						12
13						13
14						14
15						15
16						16
17						17
18						18
19						19
20						20
21						21
22						22
23						23
24						24
25						25
26						26
27						27
28						28
29						29
30						30
31						31
32						32

2.

Cash

Supplies

Accounts Payable

______________________ , *Capital*

______________________ , *Drawing*

Sales Commissions

Office Salaries Expense

Rent Expense

Automobile Expense

Supplies Expense

Miscellaneous Expense

PROBLEM 2 - 2 ___ , Concluded

3.

Trial Balance

Cash		
Supplies		
Accounts Payable		
, Capital		
, Drawing		
Sales Commissions		
Office Salaries Expense		
Rent Expense		
Automobile Expense		
Supplies Expense		
Miscellaneous Expense		

4. a. $ ______________

b. $ ______________

c. $ ______________

Name ____________________

PROBLEM 2 - 3 ___

1.

JOURNAL

PAGE *1*

	DATE		DESCRIPTION	POST. REF.	DEBIT	CREDIT	
1							1
2							2
3							3
4							4
5							5
6							6
7							7
8							8
9							9
10							10
11							11
12							12
13							13
14							14
15							15
16							16
17							17
18							18
19							19
20							20
21							21
22							22
23							23
24							24
25							25
26							26
27							27
28							28
29							29
30							30
31							31
32							32

PROBLEM 2 - 3 ___ , Continued

JOURNAL

PAGE 2

DATE		DESCRIPTION	POST. REF.	DEBIT	CREDIT

2.

ACCOUNT *Cash* ACCOUNT NO. *11*

DATE		ITEM	POST. REF.	DEBIT	CREDIT	BALANCE DEBIT	BALANCE CREDIT

ACCOUNT *Accounts Receivable* ACCOUNT NO. *12*

DATE		ITEM	POST. REF.	DEBIT	CREDIT	BALANCE DEBIT	BALANCE CREDIT

ACCOUNT *Supplies* ACCOUNT NO. *13*

DATE		ITEM	POST. REF.	DEBIT	CREDIT	BALANCE DEBIT	BALANCE CREDIT

PROBLEM 2 - 3 ___ , Continued

ACCOUNT *Prepaid Insurance* ACCOUNT NO. *14*

DATE		ITEM	POST. REF.	DEBIT	CREDIT	BALANCE DEBIT	BALANCE CREDIT

ACCOUNT *Equipment* ACCOUNT NO. *16*

DATE		ITEM	POST. REF.	DEBIT	CREDIT	BALANCE DEBIT	BALANCE CREDIT

ACCOUNT *Truck* ACCOUNT NO. *18*

DATE		ITEM	POST. REF.	DEBIT	CREDIT	BALANCE DEBIT	BALANCE CREDIT

ACCOUNT *Notes Payable* ACCOUNT NO. *21*

DATE		ITEM	POST. REF.	DEBIT	CREDIT	BALANCE DEBIT	BALANCE CREDIT

ACCOUNT *Accounts Payable* ACCOUNT NO. *22*

DATE		ITEM	POST. REF.	DEBIT	CREDIT	BALANCE DEBIT	BALANCE CREDIT

ACCOUNT , *Capital* ACCOUNT NO. *31*

DATE		ITEM	POST. REF.	DEBIT	CREDIT	BALANCE DEBIT	BALANCE CREDIT

ACCOUNT , *Drawing* ACCOUNT NO. *32*

DATE		ITEM	POST. REF.	DEBIT	CREDIT	BALANCE DEBIT	BALANCE CREDIT

ACCOUNT *Fees Earned* ACCOUNT NO. *41*

DATE		ITEM	POST. REF.	DEBIT	CREDIT	BALANCE DEBIT	BALANCE CREDIT

PROBLEM 2 - 3 ___ , Continued

ACCOUNT *Wages Expense* ACCOUNT NO. *51*

DATE		ITEM	POST. REF.	DEBIT	CREDIT	BALANCE DEBIT	BALANCE CREDIT

ACCOUNT *Rent Expense* ACCOUNT NO. *53*

DATE		ITEM	POST. REF.	DEBIT	CREDIT	BALANCE DEBIT	BALANCE CREDIT

ACCOUNT *Utilities Expense* ACCOUNT NO. *54*

DATE		ITEM	POST. REF.	DEBIT	CREDIT	BALANCE DEBIT	BALANCE CREDIT

ACCOUNT *Truck Expense* ACCOUNT NO. *55*

DATE		ITEM	POST. REF.	DEBIT	CREDIT	BALANCE DEBIT	BALANCE CREDIT

ACCOUNT *Miscellaneous Expense* ACCOUNT NO. *59*

DATE		ITEM	POST. REF.	DEBIT	CREDIT	BALANCE DEBIT	BALANCE CREDIT

Name ______________________________

PROBLEM 2-3 ___ , Concluded

3.

Trial Balance

Page not used.

Name ______________________

PROBLEM 2 - 4 ___

2. and 3.

JOURNAL

PAGE *18*

	DATE	DESCRIPTION	POST. REF.	DEBIT	CREDIT	
1						1
2						2
3						3
4						4
5						5
6						6
7						7
8						8
9						9
10						10
11						11
12						12
13						13
14						14
15						15
16						16
17						17
18						18
19						19
20						20
21						21
22						22
23						23
24						24
25						25
26						26
27						27
28						28
29						29
30						30
31						31
32						32

PROBLEM 2 - 4 ___ , Continued

JOURNAL

PAGE *19*

DATE		DESCRIPTION	POST. REF.	DEBIT	CREDIT

1. and 3.

ACCOUNT *Cash* ACCOUNT NO. *11*

DATE		ITEM	POST. REF.	DEBIT	CREDIT	BALANCE DEBIT	BALANCE CREDIT

ACCOUNT *Accounts Receivable* ACCOUNT NO. *12*

DATE		ITEM	POST. REF.	DEBIT	CREDIT	BALANCE DEBIT	BALANCE CREDIT

ACCOUNT *Prepaid Insurance* ACCOUNT NO. *13*

DATE		ITEM	POST. REF.	DEBIT	CREDIT	BALANCE DEBIT	BALANCE CREDIT

PROBLEM 2 - 4 ___ , Continued

ACCOUNT *Office Supplies* ACCOUNT NO. 14

DATE		ITEM	POST. REF.	DEBIT	CREDIT	BALANCE DEBIT	BALANCE CREDIT

ACCOUNT *Land* ACCOUNT NO. 16

DATE		ITEM	POST. REF.	DEBIT	CREDIT	BALANCE DEBIT	BALANCE CREDIT

ACCOUNT *Accounts Payable* ACCOUNT NO. 21

DATE		ITEM	POST. REF.	DEBIT	CREDIT	BALANCE DEBIT	BALANCE CREDIT

ACCOUNT *Notes Payable* ACCOUNT NO. 22

DATE		ITEM	POST. REF.	DEBIT	CREDIT	BALANCE DEBIT	BALANCE CREDIT

ACCOUNT *, Capital* ACCOUNT NO. 31

DATE		ITEM	POST. REF.	DEBIT	CREDIT	BALANCE DEBIT	BALANCE CREDIT

Name ________________________________

PROBLEM 2 - 4 ___ , Continued

ACCOUNT *, Drawing* ACCOUNT NO. *32*

DATE		ITEM	POST. REF.	DEBIT	CREDIT	BALANCE	
						DEBIT	CREDIT

ACCOUNT *Fees Earned* ACCOUNT NO. *41*

DATE		ITEM	POST. REF.	DEBIT	CREDIT	BALANCE	
						DEBIT	CREDIT

ACCOUNT *Salary and Commission Expense* ACCOUNT NO. *51*

DATE		ITEM	POST. REF.	DEBIT	CREDIT	BALANCE	
						DEBIT	CREDIT

ACCOUNT *Rent Expense* ACCOUNT NO. *52*

DATE		ITEM	POST. REF.	DEBIT	CREDIT	BALANCE	
						DEBIT	CREDIT

PROBLEM 2 - 4 ___ , Continued

ACCOUNT *Advertising Expense* ACCOUNT NO. *53*

DATE		ITEM	POST. REF.	DEBIT	CREDIT	BALANCE	
						DEBIT	CREDIT

ACCOUNT *Automobile Expense* ACCOUNT NO. *54*

DATE		ITEM	POST. REF.	DEBIT	CREDIT	BALANCE	
						DEBIT	CREDIT

ACCOUNT *Miscellaneous Expense* ACCOUNT NO. *59*

DATE		ITEM	POST. REF.	DEBIT	CREDIT	BALANCE	
						DEBIT	CREDIT

Name ____________________

PROBLEM 2 - 4 ___ , Concluded

4.

Trial Balance

Page not used.

Name ______________________________

PROBLEM 2 - 5 ___

JOURNAL

PAGE *19*

DATE	DESCRIPTION	POST. REF.	DEBIT	CREDIT
19— *Mar.* 1	*Rent Expense*	*54*	*1540 00*	
	Cash	*11*		*1540 00*
4	*Supplies*	*12*	*149 00*	
	Accounts Payable	*22*		*149 00*
6	*Advertising Expense*	*53*	*275 00*	
	Cash	*11*		*275 00*
8	*Cash*	*11*	*1595 30*	
	Service Revenue	*41*		*1595 30*
9	*Prepaid Insurance*	*13*	*144 00*	
	Cash	*11*		*144 00*
10	*Land*	*16*	*12000 00*	
	Cash	*11*		*5500 00*
	Notes Payable	*21*		*6500 00*
13	*Accounts Payable*	*22*	*847 20*	
	Cash	*11*		*847 20*
14	*Miscellaneous Expense*	*58*	*162 10*	
	Cash	*11*		*162 10*
15	*Wages Expense*	*51*	*1128 60*	
	Cash	*11*		*1128 60*
15	*Cash*	*11*	*1785 50*	
	Service Revenue	*41*		*1785 50*
16	*Ann Duncan, Drawing*	*32*	*750 00*	
	Cash	*11*		*750 00*

PROBLEM 2 - 5 ___ , Continued

JOURNAL

PAGE *20*

DATE		DESCRIPTION	POST. REF.	DEBIT	CREDIT
19— Mar.	17	Supplies	12	212 60	
		Accounts Payable	22		212 60
	20	Cash	11	1662 20	
		Service Revenue	41		1662 20
	22	Accounts Payable	22	74 20	
		Supplies	12		74 20
	25	Miscellaneous Expense	58	121 40	
		Cash	11		121 40
	25	Cash	11	1681 30	
		Service Revenue	41		1681 30
	30	Utilities Expense	52	436 60	
		Cash	11		436 60
	31	Wages Expense	51	1890 00	
		Cash	11		1890 00
	31	Ann Duncan, Drawing	32	600 00	
		Cash	11		600 00
	31	Cash	11	1276 10	
		Service Revenue	41		1276 10
6.					

Name ____________________

PROBLEM 2 - 5 ___ , Continued

1. and 3.

ACCOUNT *Cash* ACCOUNT NO. *11*

DATE		ITEM	POST. REF.	DEBIT	CREDIT	BALANCE DEBIT	BALANCE CREDIT
19— Mar.	1	Balance	✓			13,810.50	
	1		19		1,540.00		
	6		19		275.00		
	8		19	1,595.30			
	9		19		144.00		
	10		19		5,500.00		
	13		19		847.20		
	14		19		162.10		
	15		19		1,128.60		
	15		19	1,875.50			
	16		19		750.00		
	20		20	1,662.20			
	25		20		121.40		
	25		20	1,681.30			
	30		20		436.60		
	31		20		1,890.00		
	31		20		600.00		
	31		20	1,276.10		8,506.00	

ACCOUNT *Supplies* ACCOUNT NO. *12*

DATE		ITEM	POST. REF.	DEBIT	CREDIT	BALANCE DEBIT	BALANCE CREDIT
19— Mar.	1	Balance	✓			710.50	
	4		19	149.00			
	17		20	212.60			
	22		20		74.20	897.90	

ACCOUNT *Prepaid Insurance* ACCOUNT NO. *13*

DATE		ITEM	POST. REF.	DEBIT	CREDIT	BALANCE DEBIT	BALANCE CREDIT
19— Mar.	1	Balance	✓			251.50	
	9		19	144.00		395.50	

PROBLEM 2 - 5___ , Continued

ACCOUNT *Land* ACCOUNT NO. *16*

DATE		ITEM	POST. REF.	DEBIT	CREDIT	BALANCE DEBIT	BALANCE CREDIT
19— Mar.	1	Balance	✓	4625 00		4625 00	
	10		19	12000 00		16625 00	

ACCOUNT *Notes Payable* ACCOUNT NO. *21*

DATE		ITEM	POST. REF.	DEBIT	CREDIT	BALANCE DEBIT	BALANCE CREDIT
19— Mar.	10		19		6500 00		6500 00

ACCOUNT *Accounts Payable* ACCOUNT NO. *22*

DATE		ITEM	POST. REF.	DEBIT	CREDIT	BALANCE DEBIT	BALANCE CREDIT
19— Mar.	1	Balance	✓				1637 30
	4		19		149 00		
	13		19	847 20			
	17		20		212 60		
	22		20	74 20			1077 50

ACCOUNT *Ann Duncan, Capital* ACCOUNT NO. *31*

DATE		ITEM	POST. REF.	DEBIT	CREDIT	BALANCE DEBIT	BALANCE CREDIT
19— Mar.	1	Balance	✓				17760 20

Name ______________________________

PROBLEM 2 - 5 ___ , Continued

ACCOUNT *Ann Duncan, Drawing* ACCOUNT NO. *32*

DATE		ITEM	POST. REF.	DEBIT	CREDIT	BALANCE DEBIT	BALANCE CREDIT
19— Mar.	16		19	750 00			
	31		20	600 00		1,350 00	

ACCOUNT *Service Revenue* ACCOUNT NO. *41*

DATE		ITEM	POST. REF.	DEBIT	CREDIT	BALANCE DEBIT	BALANCE CREDIT
19— Mar.	8		19		1,595 30		
	15		19		1,785 50		
	20		20		1,662 20		
	25		20		1,681 30		
	31		20		276 10		7,000 40

ACCOUNT *Wages Expense* ACCOUNT NO. *51*

DATE		ITEM	POST. REF.	DEBIT	CREDIT	BALANCE DEBIT	BALANCE CREDIT
19— Mar.	15		19	1,128 60			
	31		20	1,890 00		3,018 60	

PROBLEM 2-5 ___, Continued

ACCOUNT *Utilities Expense* ACCOUNT NO. *52*

DATE		ITEM	POST. REF.	DEBIT	CREDIT	BALANCE DEBIT	BALANCE CREDIT
19— Mar.	30		20	4,366.00		4,366.00	

ACCOUNT *Advertising Expense* ACCOUNT NO. *53*

DATE		ITEM	POST. REF.	DEBIT	CREDIT	BALANCE DEBIT	BALANCE CREDIT
19— Mar.	6		19	275.00		275.00	

ACCOUNT *Rent Expense* ACCOUNT NO. *54*

DATE		ITEM	POST. REF.	DEBIT	CREDIT	BALANCE DEBIT	BALANCE CREDIT
19— Mar.	1		19	1,540.00		1,540.00	

ACCOUNT *Miscellaneous Expense* ACCOUNT NO. *58*

DATE		ITEM	POST. REF.	DEBIT	CREDIT	BALANCE DEBIT	BALANCE CREDIT
19— Mar.	14		19	162.10		162.10	
	25		20	121.40		283.50	

Name ______________________________

PROBLEM 2 - 5 ___ , Continued

DUNCAN TV REPAIR

Trial Balance

March 31, 19—

Cash	8,506.00	
Supplies	897.90	
Prepaid Insurance	395.50	
Land	16,625.00	
Notes Payable		6,500.00
Accounts Payable		1,077.50
Ann Duncan, Capital		17,760.20
Ann Duncan, Drawing	1,350.00	
Service Revenue		7,000.40
Wages Expense	3,018.60	
Utilities Expense	4,366.00	
Advertising Expense	275.00	
Miscellaneous Expense		283.50
	38,434.00	32,321.60

Verification Schedule

1. Totals of preliminary trial balance: Debit $ ______________

   Credit $ ______________

2. Difference between preliminary trial balance totals: $ ______________

3. Errors in trial balance:

4. Errors in account balances:

5. Errors in posting:

7.

DUNCAN TV REPAIR

Trial Balance

March 31, 19—

Name ______________________

PROBLEM 2-6 ___

1.

Trial Balance

Cash		
Accounts Receivable		
Supplies		
Prepaid Insurance		
Equipment		
Notes Payable		
Accounts Payable		
, Capital		
, Drawing		
Fees Earned		
Wages Expense		
Rent Expense		
Advertising Expense		
Gas, Electricity, and Water Expense		
Miscellaneous Expense		

PROBLEM 2 - 6 ___ , Concluded

2.

Name ______________________

CONTINUING PROBLEM

2. and 3.

JOURNAL

PAGE *1*

	DATE	DESCRIPTION	POST. REF.	DEBIT	CREDIT	
1						1
2						2
3						3
4						4
5						5
6						6
7						7
8						8
9						9
10						10
11						11
12						12
13						13
14						14
15						15
16						16
17						17
18						18
19						19
20						20
21						21
22						22
23						23
24						24
25						25
26						26
27						27
28						28
29						29
30						30
31						31
32						32

JOURNAL

PAGE 2

DATE	DESCRIPTION	POST. REF.	DEBIT	CREDIT

Name ______________________

CONTINUING PROBLEM, Continued

1. and 3.

ACCOUNT *Cash* ACCOUNT NO. *11*

DATE		ITEM	POST. REF.	DEBIT	CREDIT	BALANCE DEBIT	BALANCE CREDIT

ACCOUNT *Accounts Receivable* ACCOUNT NO. *12*

DATE		ITEM	POST. REF.	DEBIT	CREDIT	BALANCE DEBIT	BALANCE CREDIT

CONTINUING PROBLEM, Continued

ACCOUNT *Supplies* ACCOUNT NO. *14*

DATE		ITEM	POST. REF.	DEBIT	CREDIT	BALANCE	
						DEBIT	CREDIT

ACCOUNT *Prepaid Insurance* ACCOUNT NO. *15*

DATE		ITEM	POST. REF.	DEBIT	CREDIT	BALANCE	
						DEBIT	CREDIT

ACCOUNT *Office Equipment* ACCOUNT NO. *17*

DATE		ITEM	POST. REF.	DEBIT	CREDIT	BALANCE	
						DEBIT	CREDIT

ACCOUNT *Accumulated Depreciation--Office Equipment* ACCOUNT NO. *18*

DATE		ITEM	POST. REF.	DEBIT	CREDIT	BALANCE	
						DEBIT	CREDIT

ACCOUNT *Accounts Payable* ACCOUNT NO. *21*

DATE		ITEM	POST. REF.	DEBIT	CREDIT	BALANCE	
						DEBIT	CREDIT

Name ______________________________

CONTINUING PROBLEM, Continued

ACCOUNT *Wages Payable* ACCOUNT NO. *22*

DATE		ITEM	POST. REF.	DEBIT	CREDIT	BALANCE DEBIT	BALANCE CREDIT

ACCOUNT *Unearned Revenue* ACCOUNT NO. *23*

DATE		ITEM	POST. REF.	DEBIT	CREDIT	BALANCE DEBIT	BALANCE CREDIT

ACCOUNT *Julian Felipe, Capital* ACCOUNT NO. *31*

DATE		ITEM	POST. REF.	DEBIT	CREDIT	BALANCE DEBIT	BALANCE CREDIT

ACCOUNT *Julian Felipe, Drawing* ACCOUNT NO. *32*

DATE		ITEM	POST. REF.	DEBIT	CREDIT	BALANCE DEBIT	BALANCE CREDIT

ACCOUNT *Income Summary* ACCOUNT NO. *33*

DATE		ITEM	POST. REF.	DEBIT	CREDIT	BALANCE DEBIT	BALANCE CREDIT

CONTINUING PROBLEM, Continued

ACCOUNT *Fees Earned* ACCOUNT NO. *41*

DATE	ITEM	POST. REF.	DEBIT	CREDIT	BALANCE DEBIT	BALANCE CREDIT

ACCOUNT *Wages Expense* ACCOUNT NO. *50*

DATE	ITEM	POST. REF.	DEBIT	CREDIT	BALANCE DEBIT	BALANCE CREDIT

ACCOUNT *Office Rent Expense* ACCOUNT NO. *51*

DATE	ITEM	POST. REF.	DEBIT	CREDIT	BALANCE DEBIT	BALANCE CREDIT

ACCOUNT *Equipment Rent Expense* ACCOUNT NO. *52*

DATE	ITEM	POST. REF.	DEBIT	CREDIT	BALANCE DEBIT	BALANCE CREDIT

Name ______________________________

CONTINUING PROBLEM, Continued

ACCOUNT *Utilities Expense* ACCOUNT NO. *53*

DATE		ITEM	POST. REF.	DEBIT	CREDIT	BALANCE DEBIT	BALANCE CREDIT

ACCOUNT *Music Expense* ACCOUNT NO. *54*

DATE		ITEM	POST. REF.	DEBIT	CREDIT	BALANCE DEBIT	BALANCE CREDIT

ACCOUNT *Advertising Expense* ACCOUNT NO. *55*

DATE		ITEM	POST. REF.	DEBIT	CREDIT	BALANCE DEBIT	BALANCE CREDIT

ACCOUNT *Supplies Expense* ACCOUNT NO. *56*

DATE		ITEM	POST. REF.	DEBIT	CREDIT	BALANCE DEBIT	BALANCE CREDIT

ACCOUNT *Insurance Expense* ACCOUNT NO. *57*

DATE		ITEM	POST. REF.	DEBIT	CREDIT	BALANCE DEBIT	BALANCE CREDIT

ACCOUNT *Depreciation Expense* ACCOUNT NO. *58*

DATE		ITEM	POST. REF.	DEBIT	CREDIT	BALANCE DEBIT	BALANCE CREDIT

ACCOUNT *Miscellaneous Expense* ACCOUNT NO. *59*

DATE		ITEM	POST. REF.	DEBIT	CREDIT	BALANCE DEBIT	BALANCE CREDIT

4.

Trial Balance

Name ______________________________

PROBLEM 3 - 1 ___

1.

JOURNAL

PAGE

	DATE		DESCRIPTION	POST. REF.	DEBIT	CREDIT	
1							1
2							2
3							3
4							4
5							5
6							6
7							7
8							8
9							9
10							10
11							11
12							12
13							13
14							14
15							15
16							16
17							17
18							18
19							19
20							20
21							21
22							22
23							23
24							24
25							25
26							26
27							27
28							28
29							29
30							30
31							31
32							32

PROBLEM 3 - 1 ___ , Concluded

2.

Name ____________________

PROBLEM 3 - 2 ___

JOURNAL

PAGE ______

	DATE	DESCRIPTION	POST. REF.	DEBIT	CREDIT	
1						1
2						2
3						3
4						4
5						5
6						6
7						7
8						8
9						9
10						10
11						11
12						12
13						13
14						14
15						15
16						16
17						17
18						18
19						19
20						20
21						21
22						22
23						23
24						24
25						25
26						26
27						27
28						28
29						29
30						30
31						31
32						32

Page not used.

Name ______________________

PROBLEM 3 - 3 ___

1. *Omit "00" in the cents columns.*

MILLENNIUM SERVICES
Work Sheet
For Year Ended December 31, 19—

ACCOUNT TITLE	TRIAL BALANCE		ADJUSTMENTS		ADJUSTED TRIAL BALANCE	
	DEBIT	CREDIT	DEBIT	CREDIT	DEBIT	CREDIT
Cash	3950				3950	
Accounts Receivable	6125				7500	
Supplies	1990				850	
Prepaid Insurance	2800				750	
Equipment	40000				40000	
Accumulated Depreciation		5200				6200
Accounts Payable		3700				3700
Unearned Rent		1600				400
J. Christian, Capital		24555				24555
J. Christian, Drawing	2000				2000	
Service Revenue		49900				51275
Wages Expense	19300				20350	
Rent Expense	7200				7200	
Utilities Expense	880				880	
Miscellaneous Expense	710				710	
	84955	84955				
Supplies Expense					1140	
Insurance Expense					2050	
Depreciation Expense					1000	
Rent Income						1200
Wages Payable						1050
					88380	88380

2.

	Error (a)		Error (b)	
	Over-stated	Under-stated	Over-stated	Under-stated
1. Net income for the year would be	________	________	________	________
2. Assets at December 31 would be	________	________	________	________
3. Liabilities at December 31 would be	________	________	________	________
4. Owner's equity at December 31 would be	________	________	________	________

Name ______________________

PROBLEM 3 - 4 ___

JOURNAL

PAGE

	DATE		DESCRIPTION	POST. REF.	DEBIT	CREDIT	
1							1
2							2
3							3
4							4
5							5
6							6
7							7
8							8
9							9
10							10
11							11
12							12
13							13
14							14
15							15
16							16
17							17
18							18
19							19
20							20
21							21
22							22
23							23
24							24
25							25
26							26
27							27
28							28
29							29
30							30
31							31
32							32

Page not used.

Name ______________________________

PROBLEM 3 - 5 ___

JOURNAL

PAGE

	DATE		DESCRIPTION	POST. REF.	DEBIT	CREDIT	
1							1
2							2
3							3
4							4
5							5
6							6
7							7
8							8
9							9
10							10
11							11
12							12
13							13
14							14
15							15
16							16
17							17
18							18
19							19
20							20
21							21
22							22
23							23
24							24
25							25
26							26
27							27
28							28
29							29
30							30
31							31
32							32

Page not used.

Name ____________________

PROBLEM 3-6 ___

Work Sheet

ACCOUNT TITLE	TRIAL BALANCE		ADJUSTMENTS		ADJUSTED TRIAL BALANCE	
	DEBIT	CREDIT	DEBIT	CREDIT	DEBIT	CREDIT

PROBLEM 3 - 6 ___ , Concluded

4.

JOURNAL

PAGE

	DATE		DESCRIPTION	POST. REF.	DEBIT	CREDIT	
1							1
2							2
3							3
4							4
5							5
6							6
7							7
8							8
9							9
10							10
11							11
12							12
13							13
14							14
15							15
16							16
17							17
18							18
19							19
20							20
21							21
22							22
23							23
24							24
25							25
26							26
27							27
28							28
29							29
30							30
31							31
32							32

Name ______________________________

PROBLEM 3-7 ___

1.

JOURNAL

PAGE

	DATE		DESCRIPTION	POST. REF.	DEBIT	CREDIT	
1							1
2							2
3							3
4							4
5							5
6							6
7							
8							
9							
10							
11							
12							
13							13
14							14
15							15
16							16
17							17
18							18
19							19
20							20
21							21
22							22
23							23
24							24
25							25
26							26
27							27
28							28
29							29
30							30
31							31
32							32

PROBLEM 3 - 7 ___ , Concluded

2.

	Net Income	Total Assets	Total Liabilities	Total Owner's Equity
Reported amounts	$ ______	$ ______	$ ______	$ ______
Corrections:				
Adjustment (a)	______	______	______	______
Adjustment (b)	______	______	______	______
Adjustment (c)	______	______	______	______
Adjustment (d)	______	______	______	______
Corrected amounts	$ ______	$ ______	$ ______	$ ______

Name ______________________________

Page not used.

CONTINUING PROBLEM

	ACCOUNT TITLE	TRIAL BALANCE		ADJUSTMENTS		
		DEBIT	CREDIT	DEBIT	CREDIT	
1						1
2						2
3						3
4						4
5						5
6						6
7						7
8						8
9						9
10						10
11						11
12						12
13						13
14						14
15						15
16						16
17						17
18						18
19						19
20						20
21						21
22						22
23						23
24						24
25						25
26						26
27						27
28						28
29						29
30						30
31						31

Name ______________________

ADJUSTED TRIAL BALANCE		INCOME STATEMENT		BALANCE SHEET	
DEBIT	CREDIT	DEBIT	CREDIT	DEBIT	CREDIT

Page not used.

Name ____________________

PROBLEM 4-1 ___

1. *Use the 10-column work sheet found on pages 82-83.*
2. *Omit "00" in the cents columns.*

PROBLEM 4 - 1 ___ , Continued

	ACCOUNT TITLE	TRIAL BALANCE		ADJUSTMENTS		
		DEBIT	CREDIT	DEBIT	CREDIT	
1						1
2						2
3						3
4						4
5						5
6						6
7						7
8						8
9						9
10						10
11						11
12						12
13						13
14						14
15						15
16						16
17						17
18						18
19						19
20						20
21						21
22						22
23						23
24						24
25						25
26						26
27						27
28						28
29						29
30						30
31						31

Name ______________________________

PROBLEM 4-1 ___ , Continued

ADJUSTED TRIAL BALANCE		INCOME STATEMENT		BALANCE SHEET	
DEBIT	CREDIT	DEBIT	CREDIT	DEBIT	CREDIT

3. and 4.

JOURNAL

PAGE

DATE	DESCRIPTION	POST. REF.	DEBIT	CREDIT

JOURNAL

PAGE

	DATE		DESCRIPTION	POST. REF.	DEBIT	CREDIT	
1							1
2							2
3							3
4							4
5							5
6							6
7							7
8							8
9							9
10							10
11							11
12							12
13							13
14							14
15							15
16							16
17							17
18							18
19							19
20							20
21							21
22							22
23							23
24							24
25							25
26							26
27							27
28							28
29							29
30							30
31							31
32							32

Name ______________________

PROBLEM 4 - 2 ___

1. and 2.

JOURNAL

PAGE

	DATE		DESCRIPTION	POST. REF.	DEBIT	CREDIT	
1							1
2							2
3							3
4							4
5							5
6							6
7							7
8							8
9							9
10							10
11							11
12							12
13							13
14							14
15							15
16							16
17							17
18							18
19							19
20							20
21							21
22							22
23							23
24							24
25							25
26							26
27							27
28							28
29							29
30							30
31							31
32							32

JOURNAL

PAGE

DATE	DESCRIPTION	POST. REF.	DEBIT	CREDIT

3. *Omit "00" in the cents columns.*

4.

Name ____________________

PROBLEM 4 - 3 ___

1. *Use the 10-column work sheet found on pages 90-91.*
2.

PROBLEM 4 - 3 ___ , Continued

ACCOUNT TITLE	TRIAL BALANCE DEBIT	TRIAL BALANCE CREDIT	ADJUSTMENTS DEBIT	ADJUSTMENTS CREDIT
Cash	4507 01			
Accounts Receivable	550 00			
Supplies	1648 56			
Prepaid Insurance	790 70			
Land	20000 00			
Building	55500 00			
Accum. Depr.--Building		23400 00		
Equipment	28000 00			
Accum. Depr.--Equipment		17200 00		
Accounts Payable		5141 50		
Unearned Rent		200 00		
Tom Sawyer, Capital		61815 10		
Tom Sawyer, Drawing	2000 00			
Service Revenue		11985 67		
Wages Expense	4799 80			
Rent Expense	910 00			
Utilities Expense	728 50			
Miscellaneous Expense	307 70			
	119742 27	119742 27		

Name ______________________________

PROBLEM 4 - 3 ___ , Continued

____

____

____

	ADJUSTED TRIAL BALANCE		INCOME STATEMENT		BALANCE SHEET		
	DEBIT	CREDIT	DEBIT	CREDIT	DEBIT	CREDIT	
1							1
2							2
3							3
4							4
5							5
6							6
7							7
8							8
9							9
10							10
11							11
12							12
13							13
14							14
15							15
16							16
17							17
18							18
19							19
20							20
21							21
22							22
23							23
24							24
25							25
26							26
27							27
28							28
29							29
30							30
31							31

3.

JOURNAL

PAGE 26

DATE		DESCRIPTION	POST. REF.	DEBIT	CREDIT
		Adjusting Entries			

PROBLEM 4 - 3 ___ , Continued

4.

JOURNAL

PAGE *27*

DATE		DESCRIPTION	POST. REF.	DEBIT	CREDIT
		Closing Entries			

Name ______________________________

PROBLEM 4-3 ___, Continued

3. and 4.

ACCOUNT *Cash* ACCOUNT NO. *11*

DATE		ITEM	POST. REF.	DEBIT	CREDIT	BALANCE DEBIT	BALANCE CREDIT
1997 Jan.	1	Balance	✓			1,259.50	
	3		23		910.00	349.50	
	4		23	5,000.00		5,349.50	
	5		23		86.40	5,263.10	
	7		23	800.00		6,063.10	
	8		23	400.00		6,463.10	
	8		23		2,584.10	3,879.00	
	8		23	1,695.30		5,574.30	
	10		24		510.20	5,064.10	
	12		24		2,319.60	2,744.50	
	15		24	2,718.32		5,462.82	
	16		24		1,000.00	4,462.82	
	19		24		2,135.50	2,327.32	
	22		24		370.20	1,957.12	
	22		24	3,992.21		5,949.33	
	24		25		527.76	5,421.57	
	26		25		2,480.20	2,941.37	
	30		25		156.50	2,784.87	
	30		25		26.48	2,758.39	
	31		25		1,000.00	1,758.39	
	31		25	3,029.84		4,788.23	
	31		25		281.22	4,507.01	

PROBLEM 4 - 3 ___ , Continued

ACCOUNT *Accounts Receivable* ACCOUNT NO. 12

DATE		ITEM	POST. REF.	DEBIT	CREDIT	BALANCE DEBIT	BALANCE CREDIT
1997 Jan.	1	Balance	√	1,200.00		1,200.00	
	7		23		800.00	400.00	
	8		23		400.00	—	—
	22		24	550.00		550.00	

ACCOUNT *Supplies* ACCOUNT NO. 13

DATE		ITEM	POST. REF.	DEBIT	CREDIT	BALANCE DEBIT	BALANCE CREDIT
1997 Jan.	1	Balance	√			610.60	
	10		24	510.20		1,120.80	
	27		25	527.76		1,648.56	

ACCOUNT *Prepaid Insurance* ACCOUNT NO. 14

DATE		ITEM	POST. REF.	DEBIT	CREDIT	BALANCE DEBIT	BALANCE CREDIT
1997 Jan.	1	Balance	√			420.50	
	22		24	370.20		790.70	

ACCOUNT *Land* ACCOUNT NO. 15

DATE		ITEM	POST. REF.	DEBIT	CREDIT	BALANCE DEBIT	BALANCE CREDIT
1997 Jan.	1	Balance	√			20,000.00	

Name ______________________________

PROBLEM 4 - 3 ___ , Continued

ACCOUNT *Building* ACCOUNT NO. *16*

DATE		ITEM	POST. REF.	DEBIT	CREDIT	BALANCE DEBIT	BALANCE CREDIT
1997 Jan.	1	Balance	√			55 5 0 0 00	

ACCOUNT *Accumulated Depreciation — Building* ACCOUNT NO. *17*

DATE		ITEM	POST. REF.	DEBIT	CREDIT	BALANCE DEBIT	BALANCE CREDIT
1997 Jan.	1	Balance	√				23 4 0 0 00

ACCOUNT *Equipment* ACCOUNT NO. *18*

DATE		ITEM	POST. REF.	DEBIT	CREDIT	BALANCE DEBIT	BALANCE CREDIT
1997 Jan.	1	Balance	√			27 2 5 0 00	
	3		23	7 5 0 00		28 0 0 0 00	

ACCOUNT *Accumulated Depreciation — Equipment* ACCOUNT NO. *19*

DATE		ITEM	POST. REF.	DEBIT	CREDIT	BALANCE DEBIT	BALANCE CREDIT
1997 Jan.	1	Balance	√				17 2 0 0 00

PROBLEM 4 - 3 ___ , Continued

ACCOUNT *Accounts Payable* ACCOUNT NO. 21

DATE		ITEM	POST. REF.	DEBIT	CREDIT	BALANCE DEBIT	BALANCE CREDIT
1997 Jan.	1	Balance	√				8,625.50
	3		23		750.00		9,375.50
	8		23	2,584.10			6,791.40
	19		24	2,135.50			4,655.90
	31		25		485.60		5,141.50

ACCOUNT *Wages Payable* ACCOUNT NO. 22

DATE		ITEM	POST. REF.	DEBIT	CREDIT	BALANCE DEBIT	BALANCE CREDIT

ACCOUNT *Unearned Rent* ACCOUNT NO. 23

DATE		ITEM	POST. REF.	DEBIT	CREDIT	BALANCE DEBIT	BALANCE CREDIT
1997 Jan.	1	Balance	√		200.00		200.00

ACCOUNT *Tom Sawyer, Capital* ACCOUNT NO. 31

DATE		ITEM	POST. REF.	DEBIT	CREDIT	BALANCE DEBIT	BALANCE CREDIT
1997 Jan.	1	Balance	√				56,815.10
	4		23		5,000.00		61,815.10

Name ______________________________

PROBLEM 4 - 3 ___ , Continued

ACCOUNT *Tom Sawyer, Drawing* ACCOUNT NO. *32*

DATE		ITEM	POST. REF.	DEBIT	CREDIT	BALANCE DEBIT	BALANCE CREDIT
1997 Jan.	16		24	1 000 00		1 000 00	
	31		25	1 000 00		2 000 00	

ACCOUNT *Income Summary* ACCOUNT NO. *33*

DATE		ITEM	POST. REF.	DEBIT	CREDIT	BALANCE DEBIT	BALANCE CREDIT

ACCOUNT *Service Revenue* ACCOUNT NO. *41*

DATE		ITEM	POST. REF.	DEBIT	CREDIT	BALANCE DEBIT	BALANCE CREDIT
1997 Jan.	8		23		1 695 30		1 695 30
	15		24		2 718 32		4 413 62
	22		24		3 992 21		8 405 83
	22		24		550 00		8 955 83
	31		25		3 029 84		11 985 67

PROBLEM 4 - 3 ___ , Continued

ACCOUNT *Rent Income* ACCOUNT NO. *42*

DATE		ITEM	POST. REF.	DEBIT	CREDIT	BALANCE DEBIT	BALANCE CREDIT

ACCOUNT *Wages Expense* ACCOUNT NO. *51*

DATE		ITEM	POST. REF.	DEBIT	CREDIT	BALANCE DEBIT	BALANCE CREDIT
1997 Jan.	*12*		*24*	*2 3 1 9 60*		*2 3 1 9 60*	
	26		*25*	*2 4 8 0 20*		*4 7 9 9 80*	

ACCOUNT *Supplies Expense* ACCOUNT NO. *52*

DATE		ITEM	POST. REF.	DEBIT	CREDIT	BALANCE DEBIT	BALANCE CREDIT

ACCOUNT *Rent Expense* ACCOUNT NO. *53*

DATE		ITEM	POST. REF.	DEBIT	CREDIT	BALANCE DEBIT	BALANCE CREDIT
1997 Jan.	*3*		*23*	*9 1 0 00*		*9 1 0 00*	

Name ______________________________

PROBLEM 4-3 ___, Continued

ACCOUNT *Depreciation Expense — Building* ACCOUNT NO. *54*

DATE		ITEM	POST. REF.	DEBIT	CREDIT	BALANCE DEBIT	BALANCE CREDIT

ACCOUNT *Utilities Expense* ACCOUNT NO. *55*

DATE		ITEM	POST. REF.	DEBIT	CREDIT	BALANCE DEBIT	BALANCE CREDIT
1997 Jan.	*5*		*24*	*86 40*		*86 40*	
	30		*25*	*156 50*		*242 90*	
	31		*25*	*485 60*		*728 50*	

ACCOUNT *Depreciation Expense — Equipment* ACCOUNT NO. *56*

DATE		ITEM	POST. REF.	DEBIT	CREDIT	BALANCE DEBIT	BALANCE CREDIT

ACCOUNT *Insurance Expense* ACCOUNT NO. *57*

DATE		ITEM	POST. REF.	DEBIT	CREDIT	BALANCE DEBIT	BALANCE CREDIT

ACCOUNT *Miscellaneous Expense* ACCOUNT NO. *59*

DATE		ITEM	POST. REF.	DEBIT	CREDIT	BALANCE DEBIT	BALANCE CREDIT
1997 Jan.	30		25	26 48		26 48	
	31		25	281 22		307 70	

5.

Name ______________________________

PROBLEM 4-4 ___

1. *Use the 10-column work sheet found on pages 104 and 105.*
2. *Omit "00" in the cents columns.*

3. *Omit "00" in the cents columns.*

PROBLEM 4 - 4 ___

	ACCOUNT TITLE	TRIAL BALANCE		ADJUSTMENTS		
		DEBIT	CREDIT	DEBIT	CREDIT	
1						1
2						2
3						3
4						4
5						5
6						6
7						7
8						8
9						9
10						10
11						11
12						12
13						13
14						14
15						15
16						16
17						17
18						18
19						19
20						20
21						21
22						22
23						23
24						24
25						25
26						26
27						27
28						28
29						29
30						30
31						31

Name ____________________

PROBLEM 4 - 4 ___ , Concluded

	ADJUSTED TRIAL BALANCE		INCOME STATEMENT		BALANCE SHEET		
	DEBIT	CREDIT	DEBIT	CREDIT	DEBIT	CREDIT	
1							1
2							2
3							3
4							4
5							5
6							6
7							7
8							8
9							9
10							10
11							11
12							12
13							13
14							14
15							15
16							16
17							17
18							18
19							19
20							20
21							21
22							22
23							23
24							24
25							25
26							26
27							27
28							28
29							29
30							30
31							31

4. *Omit "00" in the cents columns.*

5. ______________ %

Name ______________________________

PROBLEM 4 - 5 ___

2. Use the 10-column work sheet found on pages 108 and 109.
3. *Omit "00" in the cents columns.*

PROBLEM 4 - 5 ___ , Continued

	ACCOUNT TITLE	TRIAL BALANCE		ADJUSTMENTS		
		DEBIT	CREDIT	DEBIT	CREDIT	
1						1
2						2
3						3
4						4
5						5
6						6
7						7
8						8
9						9
10						10
11						11
12						12
13						13
14						14
15						15
16						16
17						17
18						18
19						19
20						20
21						21
22						22
23						23
24						24
25						25
26						26
27						27
28						28
29						29
30						30
31						31

____

____

____

	ADJUSTED TRIAL BALANCE		INCOME STATEMENT		BALANCE SHEET		
	DEBIT	CREDIT	DEBIT	CREDIT	DEBIT	CREDIT	
1							1
2							2
3							3
4							4
5							5
6							6
7							7
8							8
9							9
10							10
11							11
12							12
13							13
14							14
15							15
16							16
17							17
18							18
19							19
20							20
21							21
22							22
23							23
24							24
25							25
26							26
27							27
28							28
29							29
30							30
31							31

Name ______________________

PROBLEM 4 - 5 ___ , Continued

1., 4., and 5.

ACCOUNT *Cash* ACCOUNT NO. *11*

DATE		ITEM	POST. REF.	DEBIT	CREDIT	BALANCE DEBIT	BALANCE CREDIT

ACCOUNT *Supplies* ACCOUNT NO. *13*

DATE		ITEM	POST. REF.	DEBIT	CREDIT	BALANCE DEBIT	BALANCE CREDIT

ACCOUNT *Prepaid Insurance* ACCOUNT NO. *14*

DATE		ITEM	POST. REF.	DEBIT	CREDIT	BALANCE DEBIT	BALANCE CREDIT

ACCOUNT *Equipment* ACCOUNT NO. *16*

DATE		ITEM	POST. REF.	DEBIT	CREDIT	BALANCE DEBIT	BALANCE CREDIT

ACCOUNT *Accumulated Depreciation — Equipment* ACCOUNT NO. *17*

DATE		ITEM	POST. REF.	DEBIT	CREDIT	BALANCE DEBIT	BALANCE CREDIT

ACCOUNT *Trucks* ACCOUNT NO. *18*

DATE		ITEM	POST. REF.	DEBIT	CREDIT	BALANCE DEBIT	BALANCE CREDIT

ACCOUNT *Accumulated Depreciation — Trucks* ACCOUNT NO. *19*

DATE		ITEM	POST. REF.	DEBIT	CREDIT	BALANCE DEBIT	BALANCE CREDIT

ACCOUNT *Accounts Payable* ACCOUNT NO. *21*

DATE		ITEM	POST. REF.	DEBIT	CREDIT	BALANCE DEBIT	BALANCE CREDIT

ACCOUNT *Wages Payable* ACCOUNT NO. *22*

DATE		ITEM	POST. REF.	DEBIT	CREDIT	BALANCE DEBIT	BALANCE CREDIT

ACCOUNT *, Capital* ACCOUNT NO. *31*

DATE		ITEM	POST. REF.	DEBIT	CREDIT	BALANCE DEBIT	BALANCE CREDIT

ACCOUNT *, Drawing* ACCOUNT NO. *32*

DATE		ITEM	POST. REF.	DEBIT	CREDIT	BALANCE DEBIT	BALANCE CREDIT

Name ____________________

PROBLEM 4 - 5 ___ , Continued

ACCOUNT *Income Summary* ACCOUNT NO. *33*

DATE	ITEM	POST. REF.	DEBIT	CREDIT	BALANCE DEBIT	BALANCE CREDIT

ACCOUNT *Service Revenue* ACCOUNT NO. *41*

DATE	ITEM	POST. REF.	DEBIT	CREDIT	BALANCE DEBIT	BALANCE CREDIT

ACCOUNT *Wages Expense* ACCOUNT NO. *51*

DATE	ITEM	POST. REF.	DEBIT	CREDIT	BALANCE DEBIT	BALANCE CREDIT

ACCOUNT *Supplies Expense* ACCOUNT NO. *52*

DATE	ITEM	POST. REF.	DEBIT	CREDIT	BALANCE DEBIT	BALANCE CREDIT

ACCOUNT *Rent Expense* ACCOUNT NO. *53*

DATE	ITEM	POST. REF.	DEBIT	CREDIT	BALANCE DEBIT	BALANCE CREDIT

ACCOUNT *Depreciation Expense — Equipment* ACCOUNT NO. *54*

DATE		ITEM	POST. REF.	DEBIT	CREDIT	BALANCE	
						DEBIT	CREDIT

ACCOUNT *Truck Expense* ACCOUNT NO. *55*

DATE		ITEM	POST. REF.	DEBIT	CREDIT	BALANCE	
						DEBIT	CREDIT

ACCOUNT *Depreciation Expense — Trucks* ACCOUNT NO. *56*

DATE		ITEM	POST. REF.	DEBIT	CREDIT	BALANCE	
						DEBIT	CREDIT

ACCOUNT *Insurance Expense* ACCOUNT NO. *57*

DATE		ITEM	POST. REF.	DEBIT	CREDIT	BALANCE	
						DEBIT	CREDIT

ACCOUNT *Miscellaneous Expense* ACCOUNT NO. *59*

DATE		ITEM	POST. REF.	DEBIT	CREDIT	BALANCE	
						DEBIT	CREDIT

Name ______________________________

PROBLEM 4 - 5 ___ , Continued

4. and 5.

JOURNAL

PAGE *26*

	DATE	DESCRIPTION	POST. REF.	DEBIT	CREDIT	
1		*Adjusting Entries*				1
2						2
3						3
4						4
5						5
6						6
7						7
8						8
9						9
10						10
11						11
12						12
13						13
14						14
15						15
16						16
17						17
18		*Closing Entries*				18
19						19
20						20
21						21
22						22
23						23
24						24
25						25
26						26
27						27
28						28
29						29
30						30
31						31
32						32

JOURNAL

PAGE 27

	DATE		DESCRIPTION	POST. REF.	DEBIT	CREDIT	
1			*Closing Entries (continued)*				1
2							2
3							3
4							4
5							5
6							6
7							7
8							8
9							9
10							10
11							11
12							12
13							13
14							14

6.

Name ______________________

CONTINUING PROBLEM

1. Continue with the work sheet started in Chapter 3, pages 78 and 79.
2.

Name ______________________________

3. and 4.

Note: Use the general ledger accounts provided in Chapter 2, pages 57 - 62.

JOURNAL

PAGE *3*

DATE	DESCRIPTION	POST. REF.	DEBIT	CREDIT
	Adjusting Entries			
	Closing Entries			

JOURNAL

PAGE 4

	DATE		DESCRIPTION	POST. REF.	DEBIT	CREDIT	
1			*Closing Entries (continued)*				1
2							2
3							3
4							4
5							5
6							6
7							7
8							8
9							9
10							10
11							11
12							12
13							13
14							14

Name ______________________________

COMPREHENSIVE PROBLEM 1

1. and 2.

JOURNAL

PAGE *1*

	DATE		DESCRIPTION	POST. REF.	DEBIT	CREDIT	
1							1
2							2
3							3
4							4
5							5
6							6
7							7
8							8
9							9
10							10
11							11
12							12
13							13
14							14
15							15
16							16
17							17
18							18
19							19
20							20
21							21
22							22
23							23
24							24
25							25
26							26
27							27
28							28
29							29
30							30
31							31
32							32

JOURNAL

PAGE *2*

DATE		DESCRIPTION	POST. REF.	DEBIT	CREDIT

2., 5., and 6.

ACCOUNT *Cash* ACCOUNT NO. *11*

DATE	ITEM	POST. REF.	DEBIT	CREDIT	BALANCE DEBIT	BALANCE CREDIT

ACCOUNT *Accounts Receivable* ACCOUNT NO. *12*

DATE	ITEM	POST. REF.	DEBIT	CREDIT	BALANCE DEBIT	BALANCE CREDIT

ACCOUNT *Supplies* ACCOUNT NO. *14*

DATE	ITEM	POST. REF.	DEBIT	CREDIT	BALANCE DEBIT	BALANCE CREDIT

ACCOUNT *Prepaid Rent* ACCOUNT NO. 15

DATE		ITEM	POST. REF.	DEBIT	CREDIT	BALANCE DEBIT	BALANCE CREDIT

ACCOUNT *Prepaid Insurance* ACCOUNT NO. 16

DATE		ITEM	POST. REF.	DEBIT	CREDIT	BALANCE DEBIT	BALANCE CREDIT

ACCOUNT *Office Equipment* ACCOUNT NO. 18

DATE		ITEM	POST. REF.	DEBIT	CREDIT	BALANCE DEBIT	BALANCE CREDIT

ACCOUNT *Accumulated Depreciation* ACCOUNT NO. 19

DATE		ITEM	POST. REF.	DEBIT	CREDIT	BALANCE DEBIT	BALANCE CREDIT

ACCOUNT *Accounts Payable* ACCOUNT NO. 21

DATE		ITEM	POST. REF.	DEBIT	CREDIT	BALANCE DEBIT	BALANCE CREDIT

Name ______________________________

COMPREHENSIVE PROBLEM 1, Continued

ACCOUNT *Salaries Payable* ACCOUNT NO. *22*

DATE	ITEM	POST. REF.	DEBIT	CREDIT	BALANCE	
					DEBIT	CREDIT

ACCOUNT *Unearned Fees* ACCOUNT NO. *23*

DATE	ITEM	POST. REF.	DEBIT	CREDIT	BALANCE	
					DEBIT	CREDIT

ACCOUNT *Damon Carnegie, Capital* ACCOUNT NO. *31*

DATE	ITEM	POST. REF.	DEBIT	CREDIT	BALANCE	
					DEBIT	CREDIT

ACCOUNT *Damon Carnegie, Drawing* ACCOUNT NO. *32*

DATE	ITEM	POST. REF.	DEBIT	CREDIT	BALANCE	
					DEBIT	CREDIT

ACCOUNT *Income Summary* ACCOUNT NO. 33

DATE		ITEM	POST. REF.	DEBIT	CREDIT	BALANCE DEBIT	BALANCE CREDIT

ACCOUNT *Fees Earned* ACCOUNT NO. 41

DATE		ITEM	POST. REF.	DEBIT	CREDIT	BALANCE DEBIT	BALANCE CREDIT

ACCOUNT *Salary Expense* ACCOUNT NO. 51

DATE		ITEM	POST. REF.	DEBIT	CREDIT	BALANCE DEBIT	BALANCE CREDIT

ACCOUNT *Rent Expense* ACCOUNT NO. 52

DATE		ITEM	POST. REF.	DEBIT	CREDIT	BALANCE DEBIT	BALANCE CREDIT

ACCOUNT *Supplies Expense* ACCOUNT NO. 53

DATE	ITEM	POST. REF.	DEBIT	CREDIT	BALANCE	
					DEBIT	CREDIT

ACCOUNT *Depreciation Expense* ACCOUNT NO. 54

DATE	ITEM	POST. REF.	DEBIT	CREDIT	BALANCE	
					DEBIT	CREDIT

ACCOUNT *Insurance Expense* ACCOUNT NO. 55

DATE	ITEM	POST. REF.	DEBIT	CREDIT	BALANCE	
					DEBIT	CREDIT

ACCOUNT *Miscellaneous Expense* ACCOUNT NO. 59

DATE	ITEM	POST. REF.	DEBIT	CREDIT	BALANCE	
					DEBIT	CREDIT

COMPREHENSIVE PROBLEM 1, Continued

3.

	ACCOUNT TITLE	TRIAL BALANCE DEBIT	TRIAL BALANCE CREDIT	ADJUSTMENTS DEBIT	ADJUSTMENTS CREDIT	
1						1
2						2
3						3
4						4
5						5
6						6
7						7
8						8
9						9
10						10
11						11
12						12
13						13
14						14
15						15
16						16
17						17
18						18
19						19
20						20
21						21
22						22
23						23
24						24
25						25
26						26
27						27
28						28
29						29
30						30
31						31

Name ____________________

ADJUSTED TRIAL BALANCE		INCOME STATEMENT		BALANCE SHEET	
DEBIT	CREDIT	DEBIT	CREDIT	DEBIT	CREDIT

4.

IMPACT CONSULTING

Income Statement

For Month Ended September 30, 19—

IMPACT CONSULTING

Statement of Owner's Equity

For Month Ended September 30, 19—

5.

JOURNAL

PAGE *3*

DATE		DESCRIPTION	POST. REF.	DEBIT	CREDIT
		Adjusting Entries			

6.

JOURNAL

PAGE *4*

	DATE		DESCRIPTION	POST. REF.	DEBIT	CREDIT	
1			*Closing Entries*				1
2							2
3							3
4							4
5							5
6							6
7							7
8							8
9							9
10							10
11							11
12							12
13							13
14							14
15							15
16							16
17							17
18							18
19							19
20							20
21							21
22							22
23							23
24							24
25							25
26							26
27							27
28							28
29							29
30							30
31							31
32							32

7.

IMPACT CONSULTING

Post-Closing Trial Balance

September 30, 19—

GENERAL LEDGER

2.

ACCOUNT *Accounts Receivable* ACCOUNT NO. *12*

DATE		ITEM	POST. REF.	DEBIT	CREDIT	BALANCE DEBIT	BALANCE CREDIT

ACCOUNT *Notes Receivable* ACCOUNT NO. *13*

DATE		ITEM	POST. REF.	DEBIT	CREDIT	BALANCE DEBIT	BALANCE CREDIT

ACCOUNT *Fees Earned* ACCOUNT NO. *41*

DATE		ITEM	POST. REF.	DEBIT	CREDIT	BALANCE DEBIT	BALANCE CREDIT

ACCOUNTS RECEIVABLE LEDGER

1.

NAME

ADDRESS

DATE		ITEM	POST. REF.	DEBIT	CREDIT	BALANCE

PROBLEM 5 - 1 ___ , Concluded

NAME

ADDRESS

DATE		ITEM	POST. REF.	DEBIT	CREDIT	BALANCE

NAME

ADDRESS

DATE		ITEM	POST. REF.	DEBIT	CREDIT	BALANCE

NAME

ADDRESS

DATE		ITEM	POST. REF.	DEBIT	CREDIT	BALANCE

NAME

ADDRESS

DATE		ITEM	POST. REF.	DEBIT	CREDIT	BALANCE

3. **a.** $ ______________________

b. $ ______________________

4. ______________________

Name ______________________

PROBLEM 5 - 2 ___ , Co[illegible]ued

ACCOUNTS RECEIVABLE LEDGER

2. and 4.

NAME *AGI Co.*

DATE		ITEM	POST. REF.	DEBIT	CREDIT	BALANCE
19— June	15	Balance				

NAME *Hardy Co.*

DATE		ITEM	POST. REF.	DEBIT	CREDIT	BALANCE
19— June	15	Balance				

NAME *Ross and Son*

DATE		ITEM	POST. REF.	DEBIT	CREDIT	BALANCE

NAME *Yamura Co.*

DATE		ITEM	POST. REF.	DEBIT	CREDIT	BALANCE

GENERAL LEDGER

1. and 5.

ACCOUNT *Cash* ACCOUNT NO. *11*

DATE		ITEM	POST. REF.	DEBIT	CREDIT	BALANCE DEBIT	BALANCE CREDIT
19— June	1	Balance					

ACCOUNT *Accounts Receivable* ACCOUNT NO. *12*

DATE		ITEM	POST. REF.	DEBIT	CREDIT	BALANCE DEBIT	BALANCE CREDIT
19— June	1	Balance					

ACCOUNT *Supplies* ACCOUNT NO. *14*

DATE		ITEM	POST. REF.	DEBIT	CREDIT	BALANCE DEBIT	BALANCE CREDIT
19— June	1	Balance					

ACCOUNT *Fees Earned* ACCOUNT NO. *41*

DATE		ITEM	POST. REF.	DEBIT	CREDIT	BALANCE DEBIT	BALANCE CREDIT

6.

Name ____________________

PROBLEM 5 - 3 ___ , Continued

NAME

ADDRESS

DATE		ITEM	POST. REF.	DEBIT	CREDIT	BALANCE

NAME

ADDRESS

DATE		ITEM	POST. REF.	DEBIT	CREDIT	BALANCE

NAME

ADDRESS

DATE		ITEM	POST. REF.	DEBIT	CREDIT	BALANCE

NAME

ADDRESS

DATE		ITEM	POST. REF.	DEBIT	CREDIT	BALANCE

GENERAL LEDGER

1. and 4.

ACCOUNT *Field Supplies* ACCOUNT NO. *14*

DATE		ITEM	POST. REF.	DEBIT	CREDIT	BALANCE DEBIT	BALANCE CREDIT

ACCOUNT *Office Supplies* ACCOUNT NO. *15*

DATE		ITEM	POST. REF.	DEBIT	CREDIT	BALANCE DEBIT	BALANCE CREDIT

ACCOUNT *Office Equipment* ACCOUNT NO. *18*

DATE		ITEM	POST. REF.	DEBIT	CREDIT	BALANCE DEBIT	BALANCE CREDIT

ACCOUNT *Accounts Payable* ACCOUNT NO. *21*

DATE		ITEM	POST. REF.	DEBIT	CREDIT	BALANCE DEBIT	BALANCE CREDIT

5. a. $ ______________________________

b. $ ______________________________

Name ______________________________

PROBLEM 5-4___, Continued

1. **ACCOUNTS PAYABLE LEDGER**

NAME *Aztec Supply Co.*

ADDRESS

DATE		ITEM	POST. REF.	DEBIT	CREDIT	BALANCE

NAME *Chavez Co.*

ADDRESS

DATE		ITEM	POST. REF.	DEBIT	CREDIT	BALANCE

NAME *Harper Equipment Co.*

ADDRESS

DATE		ITEM	POST. REF.	DEBIT	CREDIT	BALANCE

NAME *Heath Supply Co.*

ADDRESS

DATE		ITEM	POST. REF.	DEBIT	CREDIT	BALANCE

PROBLEM 5 - 4 ___ , Continued

2. and 3.

GENERAL LEDGER

ACCOUNT *Cash* ACCOUNT NO. *11*

DATE		ITEM	POST. REF.	DEBIT	CREDIT	BALANCE DEBIT	BALANCE CREDIT

ACCOUNT *Field Supplies* ACCOUNT NO. *14*

DATE		ITEM	POST. REF.	DEBIT	CREDIT	BALANCE DEBIT	BALANCE CREDIT

ACCOUNT *Office Supplies* ACCOUNT NO. *15*

DATE		ITEM	POST. REF.	DEBIT	CREDIT	BALANCE DEBIT	BALANCE CREDIT

ACCOUNT *Field Equipment* ACCOUNT NO. *17*

DATE		ITEM	POST. REF.	DEBIT	CREDIT	BALANCE DEBIT	BALANCE CREDIT

ACCOUNT *Office Equipment* ACCOUNT NO. *18*

DATE		ITEM	POST. REF.	DEBIT	CREDIT	BALANCE DEBIT	BALANCE CREDIT

Name ______________________________

PROBLEM 5 - 4 ___ , Continued

ACCOUNT *Land* ACCOUNT NO. *19*

DATE		ITEM	POST. REF.	DEBIT	CREDIT	BALANCE DEBIT	BALANCE CREDIT

ACCOUNT *Accounts Payable* ACCOUNT NO. *21*

DATE		ITEM	POST. REF.	DEBIT	CREDIT	BALANCE DEBIT	BALANCE CREDIT

ACCOUNT *Salary Expense* ACCOUNT NO. *61*

DATE		ITEM	POST. REF.	DEBIT	CREDIT	BALANCE DEBIT	BALANCE CREDIT

ACCOUNT *Rent Expense* ACCOUNT NO. *71*

DATE		ITEM	POST. REF.	DEBIT	CREDIT	BALANCE DEBIT	BALANCE CREDIT

4.

2., 3. and 4.

PURCHASES JOURNAL

PAGE 37

	DATE		ACCOUNT CREDITED	POST. REF.	ACCOUNTS PAYABLE CR.	MAINTENANCE SUPPLIES DR.	OFFICE SUPPLIES DR.	OTHER ACCOUNTS DR. ACCOUNT	OTHER ACCOUNTS DR. POST. REF.	OTHER ACCOUNTS DR. AMOUNT	
1	July	2	Account Payable		15680 00			Vehicles		15680 00	1
2			Browning Transportation								2
3		3	Account Payable		5360 00			Office equipment		5360 00	3
4			Gunter Computer Co.								4
5		17	Burks Co.		3200 00	3200 00				3200 00	5
6		19	McClain Co.		3260 00	3260 00					6
7					1540 00		1540 00				7
8		24	Hoy Enterprise		1020 00		1020 00				8
9											9
10											10
11											11
12											12
13											13
14											14
15											15
16											16
17											17
18											18
19											19
20											20
21											21
22											22
23											23

PROBLEM 5 - 5 ___ , Continued

CASH RECEIPTS JOURNAL

31

DATE		ACCOUNT CREDITED	POST. REF.	OTHER ACCOUNTS CR.	ACCOUNTS REC. CR.	CASH DR.
July	6	Pease Co.			3100.00	3100.00
	10	Sokol Co.			4450.00	4450.00
	12	Capps Co.			1400.00	1400.00
	16	Fees Earned		14370.00		14370.00
	18	Rent Income				1200.00
	25	Pease Co.			7280.00	7280.00
	31	Fees Earned		8300.00		8300.00

2. and 4.

REVENUE JOURNAL

PAGE 35

DATE		INVOICE NO.	ACCOUNT DEBITED	POST. REF.	ACCTS. REC. DR. FEES EARNED CR.
July	5	940	Account Receivable		1400.00
			Capps Co.		
	9	941	Account Receivable		2570.00
			Collins Co		4180.00
	11	942	Joy Co.		3490.00
	23	943	Sokol Co.		8350.00
	25	944	Collins Co.		

Name ____________________

PROBLEM 5 - 5 A, Continued

2., 3. and 4.

CASH PAYMENTS JOURNAL

34

DATE		CK. NO.	ACCOUNT DEBITED	POST. REF.	OTHER ACCOUNTS DR.	ACCOUNTS PAYABLE DR.	CASH CR.
July	1	610	Rent Expense		1,200.00		1,200.00
	6	611	Fuel Expense		750.00		750.00
	10	612	Hoy Enterprise			1,860.00	1,860.00
	10	613	Burks Co.			4,400.00	4,400.00
	11	614	Porter Co.			1,030.00	1,030.00
	13	615	Browning Transportation			15,680.00	15,680.00
	16	616	Vehicle		6,000.00		6,000.00
	18	617	Miscellaneous Administrative Expense		700.00		700.00
	20	618	Advertising Expense		2,250.00		2,250.00
	26	619	Gunter Computer Co.			5,360.00	5,360.00
	27	620	D. D. Miles, Drawing		3,000.00		3,000.00
	30	621	Driver Salaries Expense		1,400.00		1,400.00
			Office Salaries Expense		2,600.00		2,600.00
	31	622	Office Supplies		360.00		360.00

PROBLEM 5 - 5 ___ , Continued

2. and 3.

JOURNAL

PAGE *1*

	DATE		DESCRIPTION	POST. REF.	DEBIT	CREDIT	
1	July	20	Maintenance Supplies Expense		3450 00		1
2			Maintenance Supplies			3450 00	2
3							3
4							4
5							5
6							6
7							7
8							8
9							9
10							10

ACCOUNT *Cash* ACCOUNT NO. *11*

DATE		ITEM	POST. REF.	DEBIT	CREDIT	BALANCE DEBIT	BALANCE CREDIT

ACCOUNT *Accounts Receivable* ACCOUNT NO. *12*

DATE		ITEM	POST. REF.	DEBIT	CREDIT	BALANCE DEBIT	BALANCE CREDIT

Name ______________________________

PROBLEM 5 - 5 ___, Continued

ACCOUNT *Maintenance Supplies* ACCOUNT NO. *14*

DATE		ITEM	POST. REF.	DEBIT	CREDIT	BALANCE DEBIT	BALANCE CREDIT

ACCOUNT *Office Supplies* ACCOUNT NO. *15*

DATE		ITEM	POST. REF.	DEBIT	CREDIT	BALANCE DEBIT	BALANCE CREDIT

ACCOUNT *Office Equipment* ACCOUNT NO. *16*

DATE		ITEM	POST. REF.	DEBIT	CREDIT	BALANCE DEBIT	BALANCE CREDIT

ACCOUNT *Accumulated Depreciation--Office Equipment* ACCOUNT NO. *17*

DATE		ITEM	POST. REF.	DEBIT	CREDIT	BALANCE DEBIT	BALANCE CREDIT

ACCOUNT *Vehicles* ACCOUNT NO. *18*

DATE		ITEM	POST. REF.	DEBIT	CREDIT	BALANCE DEBIT	BALANCE CREDIT

PROBLEM 5 - 5 ___ , Continued

ACCOUNT *Accumulated Depreciation--Vehicles* ACCOUNT NO. *19*

DATE		ITEM	POST. REF.	DEBIT	CREDIT	BALANCE DEBIT	BALANCE CREDIT

ACCOUNT *Accounts Payable* ACCOUNT NO. *21*

DATE		ITEM	POST. REF.	DEBIT	CREDIT	BALANCE DEBIT	BALANCE CREDIT

DATE		ITEM	POST. REF.	DEBIT	CREDIT	BALANCE DEBIT	BALANCE CREDIT

ACCOUNT *D. D. Miles, Drawing* ACCOUNT NO. *32*

DATE		ITEM	POST. REF.	DEBIT	CREDIT	BALANCE DEBIT	BALANCE CREDIT

ACCOUNT *Fees Earned* ACCOUNT NO. *41*

DATE		ITEM	POST. REF.	DEBIT	CREDIT	BALANCE DEBIT	BALANCE CREDIT

ACCOUNT *Rent Income* ACCOUNT NO. *42*

DATE		ITEM	POST. REF.	DEBIT	CREDIT	BALANCE DEBIT	BALANCE CREDIT

ACCOUNT *Driver Salaries Expense* ACCOUNT NO. *51*

DATE		ITEM	POST. REF.	DEBIT	CREDIT	BALANCE DEBIT	BALANCE CREDIT

ACCOUNT *Maintenance Supplies Expense* ACCOUNT NO. *52*

DATE		ITEM	POST. REF.	DEBIT	CREDIT	BALANCE DEBIT	BALANCE CREDIT

ACCOUNT *Fuel Expense* ACCOUNT NO. *53*

DATE		ITEM	POST. REF.	DEBIT	CREDIT	BALANCE DEBIT	BALANCE CREDIT

ACCOUNT *Office Salaries Expense* ACCOUNT NO. *61*

DATE		ITEM	POST. REF.	DEBIT	CREDIT	BALANCE DEBIT	BALANCE CREDIT

PROBLEM 5 - 5 ___ , Continued

ACCOUNT *Rent Expense* ACCOUNT NO. *62*

DATE		ITEM	POST. REF.	DEBIT	CREDIT	BALANCE DEBIT	BALANCE CREDIT

ACCOUNT *Advertising Expense* ACCOUNT NO. *63*

DATE		ITEM	POST. REF.	DEBIT	CREDIT	BALANCE DEBIT	BALANCE CREDIT

ACCOUNT *Miscellaneous Administrative Expense* ACCOUNT NO. *64*

DATE		ITEM	POST. REF.	DEBIT	CREDIT	BALANCE DEBIT	BALANCE CREDIT

Name ______________________________

PROBLEM 5 - 5 ___ , Concluded

5.

6. Balance of accounts receivable controlling account: $ ____________

Balance of accounts payable controlling account: $ ____________

Page not used.

Name ____________________

PROBLEM 6 - 1 ___

JOURNAL

PAGE

	DATE		DESCRIPTION	POST. REF.	DEBIT	CREDIT	
1							1
2							2
3							3
4							4
5							5
6							6
7							7
8							8
9							9
10							10
11							11
12							12
13							13
14							14
15							15
16							16
17							17
18							18
19							19
20							20
21							21
22							22
23							23
24							24
25							25
26							26
27							27
28							28
29							29
30							30
31							31
32							32

PROBLEM 6 - 1 ___ , Concluded

JOURNAL

PAGE

	DATE		DESCRIPTION	POST. REF.	DEBIT	CREDIT	
1							1
2							2
3							3
4							4
5							5
6							6
7							7
8							8
9							9
10							10
11							11
12							12
13							13
15							15
16							16
17							17
18							18
19							19
20							20
21							21
22							22
23							23
24							24
25							25
26							26
27							27
28							28
29							29
30							30
31							31
32							32

Name ______________________

PROBLEM 6 - 2 ___

JOURNAL

PAGE ______

	DATE		DESCRIPTION	POST. REF.	DEBIT	CREDIT	
1							1
2							2
3							3
4							4
5							5
6							6
7							7
8							8
9							9
10							10
11							11
12							12
13							13
14							14
15							15
16							16
17							17
18							18
19							19
20							20
21							21
22							22
23							23
24							24
25							25
26							26
27							27
28							28
29							29
30							30
31							31
32							32

PROBLEM 6 - 2 ___ , Continued

JOURNAL

PAGE

DATE		DESCRIPTION	POST. REF.	DEBIT	CREDIT

Name ____________________

PROBLEM 6 - 2 ___ , Continued

JOURNAL

PAGE

	DATE		DESCRIPTION	POST. REF.	DEBIT	CREDIT	
1							1
2							2
3							3
4							4
5							5
6							6
7							7
8							8
9							9
10							10
11							11
12							12
13							13
14							14
15							15
16							16
17							17
18							18
19							19
20							20
21							21
22							22
23							23
24							24
25							25
26							26
27							27
28							28
29							29
30							30
31							31
32							32

JOURNAL

PAGE

	DATE	DESCRIPTION	POST. REF.	DEBIT	CREDIT	
1						1
2						2
3						3
4						4
5						5
6						6
7						7
8						8
9						9
10						10
11						11
12						12
13						13
15						15
16						16
17						17
18						18
19						19
20						20
21						21
22						22
23						23
24						24
25						25
26						26
27						27
28						28
29						29
30						30
31						31
32						32

Name ____________________

PROBLEM 6-3 ___

JOURNAL

PAGE

	DATE		DESCRIPTION	POST. REF.	DEBIT	CREDIT	
1							1
2							2
3							3
4							4
5							5
6							6
7							7
8							8
9							9
10							10
11							11
12							12
13							13
14							14
15							15
16							16
17							17
18							18
19							19
20							20
21							21
22							22
23							23
24							24
25							25
26							26
27							27
28							28
29							29
30							30
31							31
32							32

PROBLEM 6 - 3 ___ , Concluded

JOURNAL

PAGE

	DATE		DESCRIPTION	POST. REF.	DEBIT	CREDIT	
1							1
2							2
3							3
4							4
5							5
6							6
7							7
8							8
9							9
10							10
11							11
12							12
13							13
15							15
16							16
17							17
18							18
19							19
20							20
21							21
22							22
23							23
24							24
25							25
26							26
27							27
28							28
29							29
30							30
31							31
32							32

Name ______________________________

PROBLEM 6 - 4 ___

JOURNAL

PAGE

	DATE		DESCRIPTION	POST. REF.	DEBIT	CREDIT	
1							1
2							2
3							3
4							4
5							5
6							6
7							7
8							8
9							9
10							10
11							11
12							12
13							13
14							14
15							15
16							16
17							17
18							18
19							19
20							20
21							21
22							22
23							23
24							24
25							25
26							26
27							27
28							28
29							29
30							30
31							31
32							32

PROBLEM 6 - 4 ___ , Continued

JOURNAL

PAGE

	DATE	DESCRIPTION	POST. REF.	DEBIT	CREDIT	
1						1
2						2
3						3
4						4
5						5
6						6
7						7
8						8
9						9
10						10
11						11
12						12
13						13
15						15
16						16
17						17
18						18
19						19
20						20
21						21
22						22
23						23
24						24
25						25
26						26
27						27
28						28
29						29
30						30
31						31
32						32

Name ______________________________

PROBLEM 6 - 4 ___ , Continued

JOURNAL

PAGE

	DATE		DESCRIPTION	POST. REF.	DEBIT	CREDIT	
1							1
2							2
3							3
4							4
5							5
6							6
7							7
8							8
9							9
10							10
11							11
12							12
13							13
14							14
15							15
16							16
17							17
18							18
19							19
20							20
21							21
22							22
23							23
24							24
25							25
26							26
27							27
28							28
29							29
30							30
31							31
32							32

PROBLEM 6 - 4 ___ , Concluded

JOURNAL

PAGE

DATE		DESCRIPTION	POST. REF.	DEBIT	CREDIT

Name ______________________________

PROBLEM 6 - 5 ___

1. *Omit "00" in the cents columns.*

PROBLEM 6-5 ___, Continued

2. *Omit "00" in the cents columns.*

3. *Omit "00" in the cents columns.*

PROBLEM 6 - 5 ___ , Concluded

4.

Name ______________________

PROBLEM 6-6 ___

1. *Omit "00" in the cents columns.*

2. *Omit "00" in the cents columns.*

PROBLEM 6 - 6 ___ , Continued

3. *Omit "00" in the cents columns.*

Balance

Name ______________________________

PROBLEM 6-6 ___, Concluded

Sheet

Page not used.

Name ______________________________

APPENDIX PROBLEM 6 - 7 ___

1. *The 10-column work sheet form is on pages 184 or 185.*
2. *Omit "00" in the cents columns.*

APPENDIX PROBLEM 6 - 7 ___ , Continued

	ACCOUNT TITLE	TRIAL BALANCE		ADJUSTMENTS		
		DEBIT	CREDIT	DEBIT	CREDIT	
1						1
2						2
3						3
4						4
5						5
6						6
7						7
8						8
9						9
10						10
11						11
12						12
13						13
14						14
15						15
16						16
17						17
18						18
19						19
20						20
21						21
22						22
23						23
24						24
25						25
26						26
27						27
28						28
29						29
30						30
31						31
32						32
33						33
34						34
35						35
36						36
37						37

Name ______________________________

APPENDIX PROBLEM 6 - 7 ___ , Continued

	Adjusted Trial Balance		Income Statement		Balance Sheet		
	DEBIT	CREDIT	DEBIT	CREDIT	DEBIT	CREDIT	
1							1
2							2
3							3
4							4
5							5
6							6
7							7
8							8
9							9
10							10
11							11
12							12
13							13
14							14
15							15
16							16
17							17
18							18
19							19
20							20
21							21
22							22
23							23
24							24
25							25
26							26
27							27
28							28
29							29
30							30
31							31
32							32
33							33
34							34
35							35
36							36
37							37

APPENDIX PROBLEM 6 - 7 ___ , Continued

3. *Omit "00" in the cents columns.*

4. *Omit "00" in the cents columns.*

APPENDIX PROBLEM 6 - 7 ___ , Continued

5. and 6.

JOURNAL

PAGE

	DATE		DESCRIPTION	POST. REF.	DEBIT	CREDIT	
1							1
2							2
3							3
4							4
5							5
6							6
7							7
8							8
9							9
10							10
11							11
12							12
13							13
14							14
15							15
16							16
17							17
18							18
19							19
20							20
21							21
22							22
23							23
24							24
25							25
26							26
27							27
28							28
29							29
30							30
31							31
32							32

Name ______________________________

APPENDIX PROBLEM 6 - 7 ___ , Continued

JOURNAL

PAGE

	DATE		DESCRIPTION	POST. REF.	DEBIT	CREDIT	
1							1
2							2
3							3
4							4
5							5
6							6
7							7
8							8
9							9
10							10
11							11
12							12
13							13
14							14
15							15
16							16
17							17
18							18
19							19
20							20
21							21
22							22
23							23
24							24
25							25
26							26
27							27
28							28
29							29
30							30
31							31
32							32

JOURNAL

PAGE

	DATE		DESCRIPTION	POST. REF.	DEBIT	CREDIT	
1							1
2							2
3							3
4							4
5							5
6							6
7							7
8							8
9							9
10							10
11							11
12							12
13							13
14							14
15							15
16							16
17							17
18							18
19							19
20							20
21							21
22							22
23							23
24							24
25							25
26							26
27							27
28							28
29							29
30							30
31							31
32							32

Name ______________________________

COMPREHENSIVE PROBLEM 2

2., 3. and 6.

JOURNAL

PAGE *20*

	DATE		DESCRIPTION	POST. REF.	DEBIT	CREDIT	
1							1
2							2
3							3
4							4
5							5
6							6
7							7
8							8
9							9
10							10
11							11
12							12
13							13
14							14
15							15
16							16
17							17
18							18
19							19
20							20
21							21
22							22
23							23
24							24
25							25
26							26
27							27
28							28
29							29
30							30
31							31
32							32

JOURNAL

PAGE *21*

	DATE		DESCRIPTION	POST. REF.	DEBIT	CREDIT	
1							1
2							2
3							3
4							4
5							5
6							6
7							7
8							8
9							9
10							10
11							11
12							12
13							13
14							14
15							15
16							16
17							17
18							18
19							19
20							20
21							21
22							22
23							23
24							24
25							25
26							26
27							27
28							28
29							29
30							30
31							31
32							32
33							33

Name ____________________

COMPREHENSIVE PROBLEM 2, Continued

JOURNAL

PAGE *22*

DATE		DESCRIPTION	POST. REF.	DEBIT	CREDIT

JOURNAL

PAGE 23

DATE		DESCRIPTION	POST. REF.	DEBIT	CREDIT

JOURNAL

PAGE *24*

	DATE		DESCRIPTION	POST. REF.	DEBIT	CREDIT	
1							1
2							2
3							3
4							4
5							5
6							6
7							7
8							8
9							9
10							10
11							11
12							12
13							13
14							14
15							15
16							16
17							17
18							18
19							19
20							20
21							21
22							22
23							23
24							24
25							25
26							26
27							27
28							28
29							29
30							30
31							31
32							32

1., 4., and 6.

ACCOUNT *Cash* ACCOUNT NO. *110*

DATE		ITEM	POST. REF.	DEBIT	CREDIT	BALANCE	
						DEBIT	CREDIT

ACCOUNT *Notes Receivable* ACCOUNT NO. *111*

DATE		ITEM	POST. REF.	DEBIT	CREDIT	BALANCE	
						DEBIT	CREDIT

Name ______________________

COMPREHENSIVE PROBLEM 2, Continued

ACCOUNT *Accounts Receivable* ACCOUNT NO. *112*

DATE		ITEM	POST. REF.	DEBIT	CREDIT	BALANCE DEBIT	BALANCE CREDIT

ACCOUNT *Interest Receivable* ACCOUNT NO. *113*

DATE		ITEM	POST. REF.	DEBIT	CREDIT	BALANCE DEBIT	BALANCE CREDIT

ACCOUNT *Merchandise Inventory* ACCOUNT NO. *115*

DATE		ITEM	POST. REF.	DEBIT	CREDIT	BALANCE DEBIT	BALANCE CREDIT

ACCOUNT *Prepaid Insurance* ACCOUNT NO. *116*

DATE		ITEM	POST. REF.	DEBIT	CREDIT	BALANCE DEBIT	BALANCE CREDIT

ACCOUNT *Store Supplies* ACCOUNT NO. *117*

DATE		ITEM	POST. REF.	DEBIT	CREDIT	BALANCE DEBIT	BALANCE CREDIT

Name ______________________

COMPREHENSIVE PROBLEM 2, Continued

ACCOUNT *Store Equipment* ACCOUNT NO. *123*

DATE	ITEM	POST. REF.	DEBIT	CREDIT	BALANCE	
					DEBIT	CREDIT

ACCOUNT *Accumulated Depreciation—Store Equipment* ACCOUNT NO. *124*

DATE	ITEM	POST. REF.	DEBIT	CREDIT	BALANCE	
					DEBIT	CREDIT

ACCOUNT *Accounts Payable* ACCOUNT NO. *210*

DATE	ITEM	POST. REF.	DEBIT	CREDIT	BALANCE	
					DEBIT	CREDIT

ACCOUNT *Salaries Payable* ACCOUNT NO. *211*

DATE	ITEM	POST. REF.	DEBIT	CREDIT	BALANCE	
					DEBIT	CREDIT

ACCOUNT *F. R. Schwinn, Capital* ACCOUNT NO. *310*

DATE		ITEM	POST. REF.	DEBIT	CREDIT	BALANCE	
						DEBIT	CREDIT

ACCOUNT *F. R. Schwinn, Drawing* ACCOUNT NO. *311*

DATE		ITEM	POST. REF.	DEBIT	CREDIT	BALANCE	
						DEBIT	CREDIT

ACCOUNT *Income Summary* ACCOUNT NO. *312*

DATE		ITEM	POST. REF.	DEBIT	CREDIT	BALANCE	
						DEBIT	CREDIT

ACCOUNT *Sales* ACCOUNT NO. *410*

DATE		ITEM	POST. REF.	DEBIT	CREDIT	BALANCE	
						DEBIT	CREDIT

Name ______________________________

COMPREHENSIVE PROBLEM 2, Continued

ACCOUNT *Sales Returns and Allowances* ACCOUNT NO. *411*

DATE	ITEM	POST. REF.	DEBIT	CREDIT	BALANCE	
					DEBIT	CREDIT

ACCOUNT *Sales Discounts* ACCOUNT NO. *412*

DATE	ITEM	POST. REF.	DEBIT	CREDIT	BALANCE	
					DEBIT	CREDIT

ACCOUNT *Cost of Merchandise Sold* ACCOUNT NO. *510*

DATE	ITEM	POST. REF.	DEBIT	CREDIT	BALANCE	
					DEBIT	CREDIT

ACCOUNT *Sales Salaries Expense* ACCOUNT NO. 520

DATE		ITEM	POST. REF.	DEBIT	CREDIT	BALANCE DEBIT	BALANCE CREDIT

ACCOUNT *Advertising Expense* ACCOUNT NO. 521

DATE		ITEM	POST. REF.	DEBIT	CREDIT	BALANCE DEBIT	BALANCE CREDIT

ACCOUNT *Depreciation Expense* ACCOUNT NO. 522

DATE		ITEM	POST. REF.	DEBIT	CREDIT	BALANCE DEBIT	BALANCE CREDIT

ACCOUNT *Store Supplies Expense* ACCOUNT NO. 523

DATE		ITEM	POST. REF.	DEBIT	CREDIT	BALANCE DEBIT	BALANCE CREDIT

ACCOUNT *Miscellaneous Selling Expense* ACCOUNT NO. *529*

DATE		ITEM	POST. REF.	DEBIT	CREDIT	BALANCE	
						DEBIT	CREDIT

ACCOUNT *Office Salaries Expense* ACCOUNT NO. *530*

DATE		ITEM	POST. REF.	DEBIT	CREDIT	BALANCE	
						DEBIT	CREDIT

ACCOUNT *Rent Expense* ACCOUNT NO. *531*

DATE		ITEM	POST. REF.	DEBIT	CREDIT	BALANCE	
						DEBIT	CREDIT

ACCOUNT *Insurance Expense* ACCOUNT NO. *532*

DATE		ITEM	POST. REF.	DEBIT	CREDIT	BALANCE	
						DEBIT	CREDIT

ACCOUNT *Miscellaneous Administrative Expense* ACCOUNT NO. *539*

DATE		ITEM	POST. REF.	DEBIT	CREDIT	BALANCE DEBIT	BALANCE CREDIT

ACCOUNT *Interest Income* ACCOUNT NO. *611*

DATE		ITEM	POST. REF.	DEBIT	CREDIT	BALANCE DEBIT	BALANCE CREDIT

Name ______________________________

COMPREHENSIVE PROBLEM 2, Continued

Note: *The 10-column work sheet form on pages 206-207 is applicable only if following alternative instructions.*

5. *Omit "00" in the cents column.*

Income Statement

COMPREHENSIVE PROBLEM 2, Continued

	ACCOUNT TITLE	TRIAL BALANCE		ADJUSTMENTS		
		DEBIT	CREDIT	DEBIT	CREDIT	
1						1
2						2
3						3
4						4
5						5
6						6
7						7
8						8
9						9
10						10
11						11
12						12
13						13
14						14
15						15
16						16
17						17
18						18
19						19
20						20
21						21
22						22
23						23
24						24
25						25
26						26
27						27
28						28
29						29
30						30
31						31

Name ____________________

COMPREHENSIVE PROBLEM 2, Continued

Omit "00" in the cents columns.

Balance Sheet

7.

Post-Closing Trial Balance

Name ______________________________

PROBLEM 7-1 ___

PROBLEM 7 - 1 ___ , Concluded

Name ____________________

PROBLEM 7 - 2 ___

JOURNAL

PAGE

	DATE		DESCRIPTION	POST REF.	DEBIT	CREDIT	
1							1
2							2
3							3
4							4
5							5
6							6
7							7
8							8
9							9
10							10
11							11
12							12
13							13
14							14
15							15
16							16
17							17
18							18
19							19
20							20
21							21
22							22
23							23
24							24
25							25
26							26
27							27
28							28
29							29
30							30
31							31
32							32

PROBLEM 7 - 2 ___ , Concluded

JOURNAL

PAGE

	DATE		DESCRIPTION	POST REF.	DEBIT	CREDIT	
1							1
2							2
3							3
4							4
5							5
6							6
7							7
8							8
9							9
10							10
11							11
12							12
13							13
14							14
15							15
16							16
17							17
18							18
19							19
20							20
21							21
22							22
23							23
24							24
25							25
26							26
27							27
28							28
29							29
30							30
31							31
32							32

Name ______________________

PROBLEM 7 - 3 ___

JOURNAL

PAGE

	DATE	DESCRIPTION	POST REF.	DEBIT	CREDIT	
1						1
2						2
3						3
4						4
5						5
6						6
7						7
8						8
9						9
10						10
11						11
12						12
13						13
14						14
15						15
16						16
17						17
18						18
19						19
20						20
21						21
22						22
23						23
24						24
25						25
26						26
27						27
28						28
29						29
30						30
31						31
32						32

PROBLEM 7 - 3 ___ , Concluded

JOURNAL

PAGE

	DATE	DESCRIPTION	POST REF.	DEBIT	CREDIT	
1						1
2						2
3						3
4						4
5						5
6						6
7						7
8						8
9						9
10						10
11						11
12						12
13						13
14						14
15						15
16						16
17						17
18						18
19						19
20						20
21						21
22						22
23						23
24						24
25						25
26						26
27						27
28						28
29						29
30						30
31						31
32						32

Name ______________________

PROBLEM 7-4 ___

1.

PROBLEM 7 - 4 ___ , Concluded

2.

JOURNAL

PAGE

	DATE		DESCRIPTION	POST REF.	DEBIT	CREDIT	
1							1
2							2
3							3
4							4
5							5
6							6
7							7
8							8
9							9
10							10
11							11
12							12
13							13
14							14
15							15
16							16
17							17
18							18
19							19
20							20
21							21
22							22
23							23
24							24
25							25
26							26
27							27
28							28
29							29
30							30
31							31
32							32

Name ______________________________

PROBLEM 7-5 ___

1.

PROBLEM 7 - 5 ___ , Concluded

2.

JOURNAL

PAGE

DATE		DESCRIPTION	POST REF.	DEBIT	CREDIT

Name ______________________

PROBLEM 7 - 6 ___

1.

PROBLEM 7 - 6 ___ , Concluded

2.

JOURNAL

PAGE

	DATE		DESCRIPTION	POST REF.	DEBIT	CREDIT	
1							1
2							2
3							3
4							4
5							5
6							6
7							7
8							8
9							9
10							10
11							11
12							12
13							13
14							14
15							15
16							16
17							17
18							18
19							19
20							20
21							21
22							22

3. $ ______________________________

4. ______________________________

Name ____________________

PROBLEM 8-1 ___

1. and 2.

ACCOUNT *Allowance for Doubtful Accounts* ACCOUNT NO. *115*

DATE		ITEM	POST. REF.	DEBIT	CREDIT	BALANCE DEBIT	BALANCE CREDIT

ACCOUNT *Income Summary* ACCOUNT NO. *313*

DATE		ITEM	POST. REF.	DEBIT	CREDIT	BALANCE DEBIT	BALANCE CREDIT

ACCOUNT *Uncollectible Accounts Expense* ACCOUNT NO. *718*

DATE		ITEM	POST. REF.	DEBIT	CREDIT	BALANCE DEBIT	BALANCE CREDIT

2.

JOURNAL PAGE

	DATE		DESCRIPTION	POST. REF.	DEBIT	CREDIT	
1							1
2							2
3							3
4							4
5							5
6							6
7							7
8							8

JOURNAL

PAGE

	DATE	DESCRIPTION	POST. REF.	DEBIT	CREDIT	
1						1
2						2
3						3
4						4
5						5
6						6
7						7
8						8
9						9
10						10
11						11
12						12
13						13
14						14
15						15
16						16
17						17
18						18
19						19
20						20
21						21
22						22
23						23
24						24
25						25
26						26
27						27

3. $ ______________________

4. a. $ ______________________

b. $ ______________________

c. $ ______________________

1.

Year	Uncollectible Accounts Expense			Balance of Allowance Account, End of Year
	Expense Actually Reported	Expense Based on Estimate	Increase in Amount of Expense	

2.

Name ______________________

PROBLEM 8 - 3 A

JOURNAL

PAGE

DATE		DESCRIPTION	POST. REF.	DEBIT	CREDIT
Jan	11	Accounts Receivable – Atlas Co.		15000 00	
		Sales			15000 00
		Cost of Merchandise Sold		10000 00	
		Merchandise Inventory			10000 00
Mar	12	Notes Receivable – Atlas Co.		15000 00	
		Accounts Receivable – Atlas Co.			15000 00
May	11	Cash		15250 00	
		Notes Receivable – Atlas Co			15000 00
		Interest Income			250 00
June	1	Accounts Receivable – Kohl		5000 00	
		Sales			5000 00
		Cost of Merchandise Sold		3500 00	
		Merchandise Inventory			3500 00
	5	Notes Receivable – Frank Gary		7500 00	
		Cash			7500 00
	11	Cash		4900 00	
		Sales Discount		100 00	
		Notes Receivable – Kohl			5000 00
July	5	Notes Receivable – Frank Gary		7500 00	
		Cash		75 00	
		Notes Receivable – Frank Gary			7500 00
		Interest Income			75 00
Sept.	3	Cash		7675 00	
		Notes Receivable – Frank Gary			7500 00
		Interest Income			175 00
	4	Accounts Receivable – Hanover Co.		4000 00	
		Sales			4000 00
		Cost of Merchandise Sold		2500 00	
		Merchandise Inventory			2500 00
Oct.	4	Notes Receivable – Hanover Co.		4000 00	
		Accounts Receivable – Hanover Co.			4000 00

JOURNAL

PAGE

DATE		DESCRIPTION	POST. REF.	DEBIT	CREDIT
Nov.	3	Cash		4046 00	
		Notes Receivable - Hanover Co.			4000 00
		Interest Income			46 00
		Face value $4000			
		Interest on note			
		(60 days at 12%) 80			
		Maturity value $4080			
		Discount on			
		maturity value			
		(30 days at 10%) 34			
		Proceeds $4046			
Dec.	3	Accounts Receivable - Hanover Co.		4080 00	
		Cash ($4000 + $80 = $4080)			4080 00
	18	Cash		4097 00	
		Accounts Receivable - Hanover Co.			4080 00
		Interest Income			17 00
		($4080 * .1 * 15/360 = $17)			

Name ______________________________

PROBLEM 8 - 4 ___

1.

Note	(a) Due Date	(b) Interest Due at Maturity
(1)		
(2)		
(3)		
(4)		
(5)		
(6)		

2.

Note	(a) Maturity Value	(b) Discount Period	(c) Discount	(d) Proceeds	(e) Interest Expense* or Interest Income
(1)					
(2)					
(3)					
(4)					

PROBLEM 8 - 4 ___ , Concluded

3. and 4.

JOURNAL

PAGE

	DATE		DESCRIPTION	POST. REF.	DEBIT	CREDIT	
1							1
2							2
3							3
4							4
5							5
6							6
7							7
8							8
9							9
10							10
11							11
12							12
13							13
14							14
15							15
16							16
17							17
18							18
19							19
20							20
21							21
22							22
23							23
24							24
25							25
26							26
27							27
28							28
29							29
30							30
31							31
32							32

Name ____________________

PROBLEM 8 - 5 ___

JOURNAL

PAGE

DATE		DESCRIPTION	POST. REF.	DEBIT	CREDIT

JOURNAL

PAGE

DATE		DESCRIPTION	POST. REF.	DEBIT	CREDIT

Name ____________________________________

PROBLEM 9 - 1 ___

1.

Date	Purchases			Cost of Merchandise Sold			Inventory		
	Quantity	Unit Cost	Total Cost	Quantity	Unit Cost	Total Cost	Quantity	Unit Cost	Total Cost

PROBLEM 9 - 1 ___ , Concluded

2.

JOURNAL

PAGE

	DATE		DESCRIPTION	POST. REF.	DEBIT	CREDIT	
1							1
2							2
3							3
4							4
5							5
6							6
7							7
8							8
9							9
10							10
11							11
12							12
13							13
14							14
15							15
16							16
17							17
18							18
19							19
20							20
21							21
22							22
23							23
24							24
25							25
26							26
27							27
28							28
29							29

3. $ ______________________________

Name ______________________

PROBLEM 9 - 2 ___

1.

Date	Purchases			Cost of Merchandise Sold			Inventory		
	Quantity	Unit Cost	Total Cost	Quantity	Unit Cost	Total Cost	Quantity	Unit Cost	Total Cost

PROBLEM 9 - 2 ___ , Concluded

2.

Name ____________________

PROBLEM 9 - 3 ___

1. FIRST-IN, FIRST-OUT METHOD

Model	Quantity	Unit Cost	Total Cost

2. LAST-IN, FIRST-OUT METHOD

Model	Quantity	Unit Cost	Total Cost

3. AVERAGE COST METHOD

Model	Quantity	Unit Cost	Total Cost

4.a.

b.

Name ____________________

PROBLEM 9-4 ___

Inventory Sheet

December 31, 19—

Description	Inventory Quantity	Unit Cost Price	Unit Market Price	Total Cost	Total Market	Total Lower of C or M
F71	~~*40*~~ *20*	*$60*	*$ 57*	*$1,200*	*$1,140*	*$1,140*
	20	*58*		*1,160*	*1,140*	*1,140*
C22	*15*		*200*			
D82	*20*		*140*			
E34	*110*		*26*			
F17	*18*		*550*			
J19	*70*		*15*			
K41	*5*		*390*			
M21	*400*		*6*			
R72	*100*		*17*			
T15	*7*		*235*			
V55	*600*		*10*			
AC2	*80*		*45*			
BB7	*10*		*425*			
BD1	*150*		*18*			
DD1	*40*		*15*			
EB2	*60*		*30*			
FF7	*35*		*28*			
GE4	*9*		*700*			

Page not used.

Name ______________________________

PROBLEM 9-5 ___

1. *Omit "00" in the cents columns.*

	Cost		Retail	

PROBLEM 9 - 5 ___ , Concluded

2.a. *Omit "00" in the cents columns.*

b. *Omit "00" in the cents columns.*

Name ________________________________

PROBLEM 10 - 1 ___

1.

Item	Land	Land Improvements	Building	Other Accounts
a.				
b.				
c.				
d.				
e.				
f.				
g.				
h.				
i.				
j.				
k.				
l.				
m.				
n.				
o.				
p.				
q.				
r.				
s.				

*Indicates receipt

2.

Name ____________________

PROBLEM 10 - 2 ___

Depreciation Expense

Year	Straight-line method	Units-of-production method	Declining-balance method
1996			
1997			
1998			
1999			
Total			

Name ____________________

PROBLEM 10 - 3 ___

a.

STRAIGHT-LINE METHOD

Year	Calculations	Depreciation Expense

b.

UNITS-OF-PRODUCTION METHOD

Year	Calculations	Depreciation Expense

PROBLEM 10 - 3 ___ , Concluded

c.

DECLINING-BALANCE METHOD

Year	Calculations	Depreciation Expense

Name ______________________

PROBLEM 10 - 4 ___

1.a.

STRAIGHT-LINE METHOD

Year	Depreciation Expense	Accumulated Depreciation, End of Year	Book Value, End of Year

b.

DECLINING-BALANCE METHOD

Year	Depreciation Expense	Accumulated Depreciation, End of Year	Book Value, End of Year

2. ______________________

PROBLEM 10 - 4 ___ , Concluded

3.

JOURNAL PAGE

	DATE		DESCRIPTION	POST. REF.	DEBIT	CREDIT	
1							1
2							2
3							3
4							4
5							5
6							6
7							7

4.

5.

JOURNAL PAGE

	DATE		DESCRIPTION	POST. REF.	DEBIT	CREDIT	
1							1
2							2
3							3
4							4
5							5
6							6
7							7

6.

Name ______________________

PROBLEM 10 - 5 ___

JOURNAL

PAGE

	DATE	DESCRIPTION	POST. REF.	DEBIT	CREDIT	
1						1
2						2
3						3
4						4
5						5
6						6
7						7
8						8
9						9
10						10
11						11
12						12
13						13
14						14
15						15
16						16
17						17
18						18
19						19
20						20
21						21
22						22
23						23
24						24
25						25
26						26
27						27
28						28
29						29
30						30
31						31
32						32

PROBLEM 10 - 5 ___ , Concluded

JOURNAL

PAGE

	DATE		DESCRIPTION	POST. REF.	DEBIT	CREDIT	
1							1
2							2
3							3
4							4
5							5
6							6
7							7
8							8
9							9
10							10
11							11
12							12
13							13
14							14
15							15
16							16
17							17
18							18
19							19
20							20
21							21
22							22
23							23
24							24
25							25
26							26
27							27
28							28
29							29
30							30
31							31
32							32

Name ______________________________

PROBLEM 10 - 6 ___

JOURNAL

PAGE

	DATE	DESCRIPTION	POST. REF.	DEBIT	CREDIT	
1						1
2						2
3						3
4						4
5						5
6						6
7						7
8						8
9						9
10						10
11						11
12						12
13						13
14						14
15						15
16						16
17						17
18						18
19						19
20						20
21						21
22						22
23						23
24						24
25						25
26						26
27						27
28						28
29						29
30						30
31						31
32						32

PROBLEM 10 - 6 ___ , Continued

JOURNAL

PAGE

	DATE		DESCRIPTION	POST. REF.	DEBIT	CREDIT	
1							1
2							2
3							3
4							4
5							5
6							6
7							7
8							8
9							9
10							10
11							11
12							12
13							13
14							14
15							15
16							16
17							17
18							18
19							19
20							20
21							21
22							22
23							23
24							24
25							25
26							26
27							27
28							28
29							29
30							30
31							31
32							32

Name ______________________________

PROBLEM 10 - 6 ___ , Continued

ACCOUNT *Delivery Equipment* ACCOUNT NO. *122*

DATE		ITEM	POST. REF.	DEBIT	CREDIT	BALANCE	
						DEBIT	CREDIT

ACCOUNT *Accumulated Depreciation—Delivery Equipment* ACCOUNT NO. *123*

DATE		ITEM	POST. REF.	DEBIT	CREDIT	BALANCE	
						DEBIT	CREDIT

PROBLEM 10 - 6 ___ , Concluded

ACCOUNT *Depreciation Expense—Delivery Equipment* ACCOUNT NO. *616*

DATE	ITEM	POST. REF.	DEBIT	CREDIT	BALANCE DEBIT	BALANCE CREDIT

ACCOUNT *Truck Repair Expense* ACCOUNT NO. *617*

DATE	ITEM	POST. REF.	DEBIT	CREDIT	BALANCE DEBIT	BALANCE CREDIT

ACCOUNT *Gain on Disposal of Plant Assets* ACCOUNT NO. *812*

DATE	ITEM	POST. REF.	DEBIT	CREDIT	BALANCE DEBIT	BALANCE CREDIT

Name ______________________________

PROBLEM 10 - 7 ___

1., 2. and 3.

JOURNAL

PAGE

DATE		DESCRIPTION	POST. REF.	DEBIT	CREDIT

GENERAL LEDGER

ACCOUNT *Printing Equipment* ACCOUNT NO. *125*

DATE		ITEM	POST. REF.	DEBIT	CREDIT	BALANCE DEBIT	BALANCE CREDIT
1996 Jan.	1	Balance	√			527 6 5 0 00	

ACCOUNT *Accumulated Depreciation—Printing Equipment* ACCOUNT NO. *126*

DATE		ITEM	POST. REF.	DEBIT	CREDIT	BALANCE DEBIT	BALANCE CREDIT
1996 Jan.	1	Balance	√				205 7 0 0 00

Name ______________________________

PROBLEM 10 - 7 ___ , Continued

PRINTING EQUIPMENT LEDGER

PLANT ASSET RECORD ACCOUNT NO. *125-30*

ITEM *Linotype* GENERAL LEDGER ACCOUNT *Printing Equipment*

SERIAL NO. *3176P* DESCRIPTION *Model 71*

FROM WHOM PURCHASED *Murphy Equipment Co.*

ESTIMATED LIFE *10 years* ESTIMATED SCRAP OR TRADE-IN VALUE *$3,000* DEPRECIATION PER YEAR *$4,700*

DATE			EXPLANATION	ASSET			ACCUMULATED DEPRECIATION			BOOK VALUE
MO.	DAY	YR.		DEBIT	CREDIT	BALANCE	DEBIT	CREDIT	BALANCE	
10	2	89		50,000		50,000				50,000
12	31	90						1,175	1,175	48,825
12	31	91						4,700	5,875	44,125
12	31	92						4,700	10,575	39,425
12	31	93						4,700	15,275	34,725
12	31	94						4,700	19,975	30,025
12	31	95						4,700	24,675	25,325

PLANT ASSET RECORD ACCOUNT NO. *125-31*

ITEM *Press* GENERAL LEDGER ACCOUNT *Printing Equipment*

SERIAL NO. *51 X3* DESCRIPTION *Flatbed Model G3*

FROM WHOM PURCHASED *Cuthbert Press Co.*

ESTIMATED LIFE *8 years* ESTIMATED SCRAP OR TRADE-IN VALUE *$2,000* DEPRECIATION PER YEAR *$5,000*

DATE			EXPLANATION	ASSET			ACCUMULATED DEPRECIATION			BOOK VALUE
MO.	DAY	YR.		DEBIT	CREDIT	BALANCE	DEBIT	CREDIT	BALANCE	
10	1	91		42,000		42,000				42,000
12	31	92						1,250	1,250	40,750
12	31	93						5,000	6,250	35,750
12	31	94						5,000	11,250	30,750
12	31	95						5,000	16,250	25,750

PROBLEM 10 - 7 ___ , Concluded

PLANT ASSET RECORD ACCOUNT NO. 125-32

ITEM ________ GENERAL LEDGER ACCOUNT ________

SERIAL NO. ________ DESCRIPTION ________

FROM WHOM PURCHASED ________

ESTIMATED LIFE ________ ESTIMATED SCRAP OR TRADE-IN VALUE ________ DEPRECIATION PER YEAR ________

DATE			EXPLANATION	ASSET			ACCUMULATED DEPRECIATION			BOOK VALUE
MO.	DAY	YR.		DEBIT	CREDIT	BALANCE	DEBIT	CREDIT	BALANCE	

PLANT ASSET RECORD ACCOUNT NO. 125-33

ITEM ________ GENERAL LEDGER ACCOUNT ________

SERIAL NO. ________ DESCRIPTION ________

FROM WHOM PURCHASED ________

ESTIMATED LIFE ________ ESTIMATED SCRAP OR TRADE-IN VALUE ________ DEPRECIATION PER YEAR ________

DATE			EXPLANATION	ASSET			ACCUMULATED DEPRECIATION			BOOK VALUE
MO.	DAY	YR.		DEBIT	CREDIT	BALANCE	DEBIT	CREDIT	BALANCE	

4. Depreciation of the rotary press: **a.** 1997 $________ **b.** 1998 $________

Name ____________________

PROBLEM 10 - 8 ___

1.

2.

JOURNAL

PAGE

	DATE		DESCRIPTION	POST. REF.	DEBIT	CREDIT	
1							1
2							2
3							3
4							4
5							5
6							6
7							7
8							8
9							9
10							10
11							11
12							12

Page not used.

Name ______________________________

APPENDIX PROBLEM 10 - 9 ___

APPENDIX PROBLEM 10 - 10 ___

Name ______________________________

PROBLEM 11 - 1 ___

1. and 2.

JOURNAL

PAGE

	DATE		DESCRIPTION	POST. REF.	DEBIT	CREDIT	
1							1
2							2
3							3
4							4
5							5
6							6
7							7
8							8
9							9
10							10
11							11
12							12
13							13
14							14
15							15
16							16
17							17
18							18
19							19
20							20
21							21
22							22
23							23
24							24
25							25
26							26
27							27
28							28
29							29
30							30
31							31
32							32

PROBLEM 11 - 1 ___ , Concluded

JOURNAL

PAGE

	DATE		DESCRIPTION	POST. REF.	DEBIT	CREDIT	
1							1
2							2
3							3
4							4
5							5
6							6
7							7
8							8
9							9
10							10
11							11
12							12
13							13
14							14
15							15
16							16
17							17
18							18
19							19
20							20
21							21
22							22
23							23
24							24
25							25
26							26
27							27
28							28
29							29
30							30
31							31
32							32

Name ____________________

PROBLEM 11 - 2 ___

PAYROLL FOR WEEK ENDING *December 12, 1996*

NAME	TOTAL HOURS	EARNINGS			DEDUCTIONS				PAID		ACCOUNTS DEBITED		
		REGULAR	OVER-TIME	TOTAL	FICA TAX	FEDERAL INCOME TAX	MEDICAL INS.	TOTAL	NET AMOUNT	CK. NO.	SALES SALARIES EXPENSE	OFFICE SALARIES EXPENSE	DELIVERY SALARIES EXPENSE
Arnold, James	42.00	$ 640.00	$ 48.00	$ 688.00	$ 51.60	$ 97.00	$ 28.20	$ 176.80	$ 511.20	632	688.00		
Christy, Howard	46.00	800.00	180.00	980.00	73.50	140.00	46.70	260.20	719.80	633	980.00		
Davis, Lyn	40.00	640.00		640.00	48.00	83.00	26.30	157.30	482.70	634			640.00
Gunwald, Jenny		1,340.00		1,340.00	100.50	281.00	85.00	466.50	873.50	635		1,340.00	
Jenkins, Sara	48.00	800.00	240.00	1,040.00	78.00	115.00	45.00	238.00	802.00	636	1,040.00		
Ouchi, T.		1,680.00		1,680.00	126.00	405.00	95.00	626.00	1,054.00	637		1,680.00	
Peters, Ken	54.00	320.00	168.00	488.00	36.60	28.00	16.20	80.80	407.20	638	488.00		
Raines, Frank	40.00	480.00		480.00	36.00	75.00	24.50	135.50	344.50	639			480.00
Wilson, T. J.	30.00	420.00		420.00	31.50	70.00	18.10	119.60	300.40	640			420.00
		$7,120.00	$636.00	$7,756.00	$581.70	$1,294.00	$385.00	$2,260.70	$5,495.30		$3,196.00	$3,020.00	$1,540.00

PROBLEM 11 - 2 ___ , Concluded

JOURNAL

PAGE

DATE		DESCRIPTION	POST. REF.	DEBIT	CREDIT

Name ______________________________

PROBLEM 11 - 3 ___

1.

Employee	Gross Earnings	Federal Income Tax Withheld	FICA Tax Withheld

2. Payroll taxes incurred and paid by employer:

a. FICA . . . . $ ______________

b. State unemployment compensation . . . . ______________

c. Federal unemployment compensation . . . . ______________

d. Total . . . . $ ______________

Page not used.

Name ______________________________

PROBLEM 11 - 4 ___

1. *The payroll register form is on pages 272 and 273.*

2.

JOURNAL

PAGE

DATE	DESCRIPTION	POST. REF.	DEBIT	CREDIT

PROBLEM 11 - 4 ___ , Continued

1. **PAYROLL FOR WEEK ENDING**

	NAME	TOTAL HOURS	EARNINGS			DEDUCTIONS		
			REGULAR	OVERTIME	TOTAL	FICA TAX	FEDERAL INCOME TAX	
1								1
2								2
3								3
4								4
5								5
6								6
7								7
8								8
9								9
10								10
11								11
12								12
13								13
14								14
15								15
16								16
17								17
18								18
19								19
20								20
21								21
22								22
23								23
24								24
25								25
26								26
27								27
28								28
29								29
30								30
31								31
32								32

Name ____________________

PROBLEM 11 - 4 ___ , Concluded

December 7, 1997

			PAID		ACCOUNTS DEBITED		
	U.S. SAVINGS BONDS	TOTAL	NET AMOUNT	CK. NO.	SALES SALARIES EXPENSE	OFFICE SALARIES EXPENSE	
1							1
2							2
3							3
4							4
5							5
6							6
7							7
8							8
9							9
10							10
11							11
12							12
13							13
14							14
15							15
16							16
17							17
18							18
19							19
20							20
21							21
22							22
23							23
24							24
25							25
26							26
27							27
28							28
29							29
30							30
31							31
32							32

Page not used.

Name ____________________

PROBLEM 11 - 5 ___

1. and 2.

JOURNAL

PAGE

	DATE		DESCRIPTION	POST. REF.	DEBIT	CREDIT	
1							1
2							2
3							3
4							4
5							5
6							6
7							7
8							8
9							9
10							10
11							11
12							12
13							13
14							14
15							15
16							16
17							17
18							18
19							19
20							20
21							21
22							22
23							23
24							24
25							25
26							26
27							27
28							28
29							29
30							30
31							31
32							32

PROBLEM 11 - 5 ___ , Concluded

JOURNAL

PAGE

DATE		DESCRIPTION	POST. REF.	DEBIT	CREDIT

Name ____________________

PROBLEM 11 - 6 ___

1., 2. and 3.

JOURNAL

PAGE

DATE		DESCRIPTION	POST. REF.	DEBIT	CREDIT

PROBLEM 11 - 6 ___ , Concluded

JOURNAL

PAGE

	DATE		DESCRIPTION	POST. REF.	DEBIT	CREDIT	
1							1
2							2
3							3
4							4
5							5
6							6
7							7
8							8
9							9
10							10
11							11
12							12
13							13
14							14
15							15
16							16
17							17
18							18
19							19
20							20
21							21
22							22
23							23
24							24
25							25
26							26
27							27
28							29
29							29

4. $ ________________________________

Name ____________________

COMPREHENSIVE PROBLEM 3

1.

JOURNAL

PAGE ______

	DATE	DESCRIPTION	POST. REF.	DEBIT	CREDIT	
1						1
2						2
3						3
4						4
5						5
6						6
7						7
8						8
9						9
10						10
11						11
12						12
13						13
14						14
15						15
16						16
17						17
18						18
19						19
20						20
21						21
22						22
23						23
24						24
25						25
26						26
27						27
28						28
29						29
30						30
31						31
32						32

JOURNAL

PAGE

	DATE	DESCRIPTION	POST. REF.	DEBIT	CREDIT	
1						1
2						2
3						3
4						4
5						5
6						6
7						7
8						8
9						9
10						10
11						11
12						12
13						13
14						14
15						15
16						16
17						17
18						18
19						19
20						20
21						21
22						22
23						23
24						24
25						25
26						26
27						27
28						28
29						29
30						30
31						31
32						32

Name ______________________________

COMPREHENSIVE PROBLEM 3 , Continued

JOURNAL

PAGE

	DATE	DESCRIPTION	POST. REF.	DEBIT	CREDIT	
1						1
2						2
3						3
4						4
5						5
6						6
7						7
8						8
9						9
10						10
11						11
12						12
13						13
14						14
15						15
16						16
17						17
18						18
19						19
20						20
21						21
22						22
23						23
24						24
25						25
26						26
27						27
28						28
29						29
30						30
31						31
32						32

COMPREHENSIVE PROBLEM 3, Continued

2.

Bank Reconciliation

Name ______________________________

COMPREHENSIVE PROBLEM 3 , Continued

3. and 4.

JOURNAL

PAGE

	DATE		DESCRIPTION	POST. REF.	DEBIT	CREDIT	
1							1
2							2
3							3
4							4
5							5
6							6
7							7
8							8
9							9
10							10
11							11
12							12
13							13
14							14
15							15
16							16
17							17
18							18
19							19
20							20
21							21
22							22
23							23
24							24
25							25
26							26
27							27
28							28
29							29
30							30
31							31
32							32

JOURNAL

PAGE

DATE		DESCRIPTION	POST. REF.	DEBIT	CREDIT

5. *Omit "00" in the cents columns.*

Balance Sheet

6.

Page not used.

Name ______________________________

PROBLEM 12 - 1 ___

1. Gross profit percentages:

First year ______________________________

Second year ______________________________

Third year ______________________________

2. *Omit "00" in the cents columns.*

	FIRST YEAR	SECOND YEAR	THIRD YEAR

Page not used.

Name ____________________

PROBLEM 12-2 ___

1. and 2.

PROBLEM 12 - 2 ___ , Concluded

3.

Name ______________________________

PROBLEM 12 - 3 ___

Omit "00" in the cents columns.

	1996	1997	1998

Page not used.

Name ______________________________

PROBLEM 12 - 4 ___

Omit "00" in the cents columns.

	FIRST YEAR	SECOND YEAR	THIRD YEAR
Net income reported			
Increase (decrease) in net income attribut-			
able to change in method of determining:			
Uncollectible accounts expense			
Ending merchandise inventory			
Depreciation expense			
Total			
Net income as recomputed			

Page not used.

Name ____________________

PROBLEM 12 - 5 ___

JOURNAL

PAGE

	DATE		DESCRIPTION	POST. REF.	DEBIT	CREDIT	
1							1
2							2
3							3
4							4
5							5
6							6
7							7
8							8
9							9
10							10
11							11
12							12
13							13
14							14
15							15
16							16
17							17
18							18
19							19
20							20
21							21
22							22
23							23
24							24
25							25
26							26
27							27
28							28
29							29
30							30
31							31
32							32

PROBLEM 12 - 5 ___ , Concluded

JOURNAL

PAGE

	DATE		DESCRIPTION	POST. REF.	DEBIT	CREDIT	
1							1
2							2
3							3
4							4
5							5
6							6
7							7
8							8
9							9
10							10
11							11
12							12
13							13
14							14
15							15
16							16
17							17
18							18
19							19
20							20
21							21
22							22
23							23
24							24
25							25
26							26
27							27
28							28
29							29
30							30
31							31
32							32

Name ______________________________

PROBLEM 13 - 1 ___

1. and 3.

JOURNAL

PAGE

	DATE		DESCRIPTION	POST. REF.	DEBIT	CREDIT	
1							1
2							2
3							3
4							4
5							5
6							6
7							7
8							8
9							9
10							10
11							11
12							12
13							13
14							14
15							15
16							16
17							17
18							18
19							19
20							20
21							21
22							22
23							23
24							24
25							25
26							26
27							27
28							28
29							29
30							30
31							31
32							32

PROBLEM 13 - 1 ___ , Concluded

2. *Omit "00" in the cents columns.*

Balance Sheet

Name ______________________________

PROBLEM 13 - 2 ___

PLAN	(1)		(2)	
a.				
b.				
c.				
d.				
e.				
f.				

PROBLEM 13 - 2 ___ , Concluded

Name ______________________________

PROBLEM 13-3 ___

1. *Omit "00" in the cents columns.*

Income Statement

For Year Ended December 31, 19—

PROBLEM 13 - 3 ___ , Continued

2. *Omit "00" in the cents columns.*

Statement of Owner's Equity

For Year Ended December 31, 19—

			Total

3. *Omit "00" in the cents columns.*

Balance Sheet

December 31, 19—

Page not used.

Name ____________________

PROBLEM 13 - 4 ___

1. and 2.

JOURNAL

PAGE

DATE		DESCRIPTION	POST. REF.	DEBIT	CREDIT

PROBLEM 13 - 4 ___ , Concluded

3. *Omit "00" in the cents columns.*

Balance Sheet

Name ______________________

PROBLEM 13 - 5 ___

1. *Omit "00" in the cents columns.*

Statement of Partnership Liquidation
For Period

	CASH	NONCASH ASSETS	LIABILITIES	CAPITAL		
Balances before realization						

2.

1. *Omit "00" in the cents columns.*

MENTZER, HOLDER, AND WONG
Statement of Partnership Liquidation
For Period December 1-20, 19—

	CASH	NONCASH ASSETS	LIABILITIES	CAPITAL		
				MENTZER (50%)	HOLDER (30%)	WONG (20%)
Balances before realization	16400	95000	50000	35500	9900	16000
Sale of assets and division of loss	+48000	−95000	— — —	−23500	−14100	−9400
Balances after realization	64400	0	50000	12000	4200 (Dr)	6600
Payment of liabilities	−50000	— — —	−50000	— — —	— — —	— — —
Balances after payment of liabilities	14400	0	0	12000	4200 (Dr)	6600
Receipt (Division) of deficiency						
Balances						
Distribution of cash to partners						
Final balances						

PROBLEM 13 - 6 ___ , Concluded

2.

JOURNAL

PAGE

	DATE		DESCRIPTION	POST. REF.	DEBIT	CREDIT	
1							1
2							2
3							3
4							4
5							5
6							6
7							7
8							8
9							9
10							10
11							11
12							12
13							13
14							14
15							15
16							16
17							17
18							18
19							19
20							20
21							21
22							22
23							23
24							24
25							25
26							26
27							27
28							28
29							29
30							30
31							31
32							32

Name ____________________

PROBLEM 13 - 7 ___

1. *Omit "00" in the cents columns.*

Statement of Partnership Liquidation
For Period

	CASH	NONCASH ASSETS	LIABILITIES	CAPITAL		
Balances before realization						

2. *Omit "00" in the cents columns.*

Statement of Partnership Liquidation
For Period

	CASH	NONCASH ASSETS	LIABILITIES	CAPITAL		
Balances before realization						

3. *Omit "00" in the cents columns.*

Statement of Partnership Liquidation
For Period

	CASH	NONCASH ASSETS	LIABILITIES	CAPITAL		
Balances before realization						

Page not used.

Name ______________________

PROBLEM D - 1

JOURNAL

PAGE

	DATE		DESCRIPTION	POST. REF.	DEBIT	CREDIT	
1							1
2							2
3							3
4							4
5							5
6							6
7							7
8							8
9							9
10							10
11							11
12							12
13							13
14							14
15							15
16							16
17							17
18							18
19							19
20							20
21							21
22							22
23							23
24							24
25							25
26							26
27							27
28							28
29							29
30							30
31							31
32							32

JOURNAL

PAGE

	DATE		DESCRIPTION	POST. REF.	DEBIT	CREDIT	
1							1
2							2
3							3
4							4
5							5
6							6
7							7
8							8
9							9
10							10
11							11
12							12
13							13
14							14
15							15
16							16
17							17
18							18
19							19
20							20
21							21
22							22
23							23
24							24
25							25
26							26
27							27
28							28
29							29
30							30
31							31
32							32

Name ____________________

PROBLEM D - 2

JOURNAL

PAGE ______

DATE		DESCRIPTION	POST. REF.	DEBIT	CREDIT

PROBLEM D - 2 , Concluded

JOURNAL

PAGE

	DATE		DESCRIPTION	POST. REF.	DEBIT	CREDIT	
1							1
2							2
3							3
4							4
5							5
6							6
7							7
8							8
9							9
10							10
11							11
12							12
13							13
14							14
15							15
16							16
17							17
18							18
19							19
20							20
21							21
22							22
23							23
24							24
25							25
26							26
27							27
28							28
29							29
30							30
31							31
32							32

Name ____________________

PROBLEM D - 3

1.

JOURNAL

PAGE

	DATE		DESCRIPTION	POST. REF.	DEBIT	CREDIT	
1							1
2							2
3							3
4							4
5							5
6							6
7							7
8							8
9							9
10							10
11							11
12							12
13							13
14							14
15							15
16							16
17							17
18							18
19							19
20							20
21							21
22							22
23							23
24							24
25							25
26							26
27							27
28							28
29							29
30							30
31							31
32							32

PROBLEM D - 3 , Concluded

2.

JOURNAL

PAGE

	DATE		DESCRIPTION	POST. REF.	DEBIT	CREDIT	
1							1
2							2
3							3
4							4
5							5
6							6
7							7
8							8
9							9
10							10
11							11
12							12
13							13
14							14
15							15
16							16
17							17
18							18
19							19
20							20
21							21
22							22
23							23
24							24
25							25
26							26
27							27
28							28
29							29
30							30
31							31
32							32

Name ______________________________

PROBLEM D - 4

1. *Use the 10-column work sheets found on pages 324-327.*

PROBLEM D - 4 ___ , Continued

	ACCOUNT TITLE	TRIAL BALANCE		ADJUSTMENTS		
		DEBIT	CREDIT	DEBIT	CREDIT	
1						1
2						2
3						3
4						4
5						5
6						6
7						7
8						8
9						9
10						10
11						11
12						12
13						13
14						14
15						15
16						16
17						17
18						18
19						19
20						20
21						21
22						22
23						23
24						24
25						25
26						26
27						27
28						28
29						29
30						30
31						31

Name ______________________________

PROBLEM D - 4 ___ , Continued

	ADJUSTED TRIAL BALANCE		INCOME STATEMENT		BALANCE SHEET		
	DEBIT	CREDIT	DEBIT	CREDIT	DEBIT	CREDIT	
1							1
2							2
3							3
4							4
5							5
6							6
7							7
8							8
9							9
10							10
11							11
12							12
13							13
14							14
15							15
16							16
17							17
18							18
19							19
20							20
21							21
22							22
23							23
24							24
25							25
26							26
27							27
28							28
29							29
30							30
31							31

PROBLEM D - 4 ___ , Continued

	ACCOUNT TITLE	TRIAL BALANCE		ADJUSTMENTS		
		DEBIT	CREDIT	DEBIT	CREDIT	
1						1
2						2
3						3
4						4
5						5
6						6
7						7
8						8
9						9
10						10
11						11
12						12
13						13
14						14
15						15
16						16
17						17
18						18
19						19
20						20
21						21
22						22
23						23
24						24
25						25
26						26
27						27
28						28
29						29
30						30
31						31

Name ______________________________

PROBLEM D - 4 ___ , Continued

	ADJUSTED TRIAL BALANCE		INCOME STATEMENT		BALANCE SHEET		
	DEBIT	CREDIT	DEBIT	CREDIT	DEBIT	CREDIT	
1							1
2							2
3							3
4							4
5							5
6							6
7							7
8							8
9							9
10							10
11							11
12							12
13							13
14							14
15							15
16							16
17							17
18							18
19							19
20							20
21							21
22							22
23							23
24							24
25							25
26							26
27							27
28							28
29							29
30							30
31							31

PROBLEM D - 4 ___ , Continued

2. *Omit "00" in the cents columns.*

Name ______________________________

PROBLEM D - 4 ___ , Continued

3. *Omit "00" in the cents columns.*

4. *Omit "00" in the cents columns.*

PROBLEM D - 4 ___ , Continued

5.

JOURNAL

PAGE

	DATE	DESCRIPTION	POST. REF.	DEBIT	CREDIT	
1						1
2						2
3						3
4						4
5						5
6						6
7						7
8						8
9						9
10						10
11						11
12						12
13						13
14						14
15						15
16						16
17						17
18						18
19						19
20						20
21						21
22						22
23						23
24						24
25						25
26						26
27						27
28						28
29						29
30						30
31						31
32						32

Name ______________________________

PROBLEM D - 4 ___ , Continued

6.

JOURNAL

PAGE

	DATE		DESCRIPTION	POST. REF.	DEBIT	CREDIT	
1							1
2							2
3							3
4							4
5							5
6							6
7							7
8							8
9							9
10							10
11							11
12							12
13							13
14							14
15							15
16							16
17							17
18							18
19							19
20							20
21							21
22							22
23							23
24							24
25							25
26							26
27							27
28							28
29							29
30							30
31							31
32							32

PROBLEM D - 4 , Concluded

JOURNAL

PAGE

	DATE	DESCRIPTION	POST. REF.	DEBIT	CREDIT	
1						1
2						2
3						3
4						4
5						5
6						6
7						7
8						8
9						9
10						10
11						11
12						12
13						13
14						14
15						15
16						16
17						17
18						18
19						19
20						20
21						21
22						22
23						23
24						24
25						25
26						26
27						27
28						28
29						29
30						30
31						31
32						32